THE INTEGRATION OF THE EUROPEAN UNION AND DOMESTIC POLITICAL ISSUES

WERNER J. FELD

PRAEGER

Westport, Connecticut
London

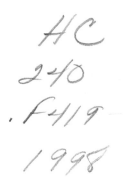

Library of Congress Cataloging-in-Publication Data

Feld, Werner J.
   The integration of the European Union and domestic political issues /
Werner J. Feld.
      p. cm.
   Includes bibliographical references and index.
   ISBN 0-275-96068-4 (alk. paper)
   1. European Union countries—Economic integration. 2. European Union
countries—Economic policy. I. Title.
HC240.F419   1998
337.1'42—dc21   97-28864

British Library Cataloguing in Publication Data is available.

Library of Congress Catalog Card Number: 97-28864
ISBN: 0-275-96068-4

First published in 1998

Praeger Publishers, 88 Post Road West, Westport, CT 06881
An imprint of Greenwood Publishing Group, Inc.

Printed in the United States of America

The paper used in this book complies with the
Permanent Paper Standard issued by the National
Information Standards Organization (Z39.48-1984).

10   9   8   7   6   5   4   3   2   1

*To
Elizabeth*

CONTENTS

FIGURES

TABLES

ACKNOWLEDGMENTS

I would like to thank Karen Norris for her outstanding assistance in preparing and typing the draft for this volume. Without her thoughtful support, the completion of the manuscript would have been much more difficult and time-consuming. I am also indebted to Robin Stearns and Dr. James T. Sabin of Greenwood Publishing Group for their valuable cooperation and assistance.

1   INTRODUCTION

The purpose of this volume is to examine the determinants of the process of regional integration among the participants of the European Union (EU). Two factors play a vital role: first, the number of participants has increased from six in 1957 (1953, if one considers the European Coal and Steel Community as the beginning) to 15 in 1997, and this number may grow further if and when East European countries such as Poland and the Czech State are given EU membership. Second, administrative changes may be made in the institutional structures of the EU that may affect the internal and external decision-making processes in the years to come.

The theoretical basis of regional integration goes back to the 1950s, and the best-known scholars in this field were E. B. Haas and Leon Lindberg. The most important names of the theories were functionalism, neo-functionalism, and intergovernmentalism. A well-documented book dealing with the period of 1950 to 1972 is Charles Pentland, *International Theory and European Integration* (New York, 1973). Following this period and especially during the late eighties and early nineties, a variety of new theoretical efforts to explain and predict regional integration sprang forward. We will use chapter 2 to provide an overview of these efforts and analyze the extent to which they explain the present and future developments in the EU integration process. What can we learn from the activities of the member state governments during the Intergovernmental Conference (IGC), and from the goals and their implementation proposed by the European Union Commission? Was the Reflection Group, consisting of representatives of the

EU member state governments, a useful exercise in smoothing the discussion and activities of the IGC?

The proceedings at the IGC may well be influenced by the understanding that existed among the member states regarding the theory of democracy, which has practical implications for possible changes in the Maastricht Treaty. This involves the European Parliament and its relation to the national parliaments and to the policy-making process for the Union internally and externally. Arriving at acceptable solutions has been difficult, and the problems are discussed in chapter 3. The evolution of the EU may depend on more extensive study of integration theory, to be combined with the democratic theory, to satisfy the political needs of the EU people and to ensure appropriate administrative rules in the EU decision-making structures to move political and economic objectives forward. A discussion of democratic theory also must include the process of national preference formation and the process of policy learning and adoption.

The short-range and long-range success of the IGC depends very much on economic and social factors. The EU is in a job crisis—with 18 million Europeans out of work and more than 50 million threatened by social exclusion—hence the EU's duty is to respond to the people's worries. These problems are discussed in chapter 4, and it should be noted that the IGC may require as long as two years to come up with some favorable conclusions.[1]

One major source of difficulty and uncertainty is the success or failure of the European Monetary Union (EMU), which depends on a variety of economic conditions—some of which are supported by several of the EU member states and the EU Commission but are opposed strongly by others on nationalistic and economic grounds.

One of the most difficult issues discussed during the IGC has been the attempt by the EU Commission and some of the member states to introduce a common currency, the "Euro," an effort that has produced strong economic arguments as well as legal and constitutional discussions. The Treaty of Maastricht, approved by all the member states in 1993, provides guidelines for the member states to assure a smooth change from national currency to the Euro, but nationalistic feelings and financial restrictions may permit only a very slow transfer from national to EU currencies. These issues are discussed in detail in chapter 5.

Important aspects of the future can be gleaned from public opinion polls, which the Commission conducts about every six months in all member states. Trends have been developed over several years. Even in Germany in 1997, the support for a common currency appears to be less than enthusiastic, despite the current chancellor's leadership role in moving toward EMU. Chapter 6 will offer a thorough analysis of opinions regarding this issue. EU-wide trends of the future include possible changes to the Maastricht Treaty, which is officially recognized as the major objective of the IGC. The IGC is a conference that was re-started at the end of March 1996 in Turin, Italy, and was moved to Dublin, Ireland, in the second half of 1996. It operated in the Netherlands in the first half of 1997 and was planned to operate in Luxembourg during the second half of that year.[2]

Public opinion can be influenced regarding individual issues, and lobbyists operating in various governmental and parliamentary institutions on EU, national, and regional levels may play significant roles. Lobbyists on the EU level—that is, in the Commission and European Parliament (EP) in particular—are becoming more influential, despite the fact that the EP has relatively little decision-making power in the EU. Efforts are being made currently to set up rules for lobbying activities. After all, the number of lobbyists operating in particular EU institutions may be seen as an indirect indicator of the expansion of the institution's influence and power. This hypothesis will be discussed in detail in chapter 6, and provides interesting insights into organizational capabilities at all levels of government in the EU.

Many of the results will depend on the extent of the changes that the IGC will accept. Depending on these changes, either the EMU will be introduced on time among a small number of initial EU member states, or the entire project may be postponed as a result of the economic views of conference participants and decision-making elites in the EU member states. Economic data will be interpreted, and the evaluation of these data is likely to vary among member state governments and publics.

Another issue that is very likely to influence the EU integration process is the evolution of a common foreign and defense policy. While progress in cooperation by member states on foreign policy matters can be observed, the rules of the Maastricht Treaty in this respect do not ensure the smooth cooperation of foreign policy decision making. Such rules include a provision for majority voting to establish and implement truly common foreign policies for all member states. Hence the IGC must discuss possible changes and improvements in this very important field. This is especially essential considering the possible further expansion of the EU membership into the east and south.

A common security and defense policy is an essential item for the future, going beyond the protection of NATO offered to the member states and affecting state decisions regarding the EU membership. There had been hopes that the Western European Union (WEU) would constitute the defense arm of the European Union, but very little progress, if any, has been made in this respect. These issues will be dealt with in detail in chapter 7, which will include a discussion of the likely move of NATO to add members in Eastern Europe such as Poland and the Czech State.

Chapter 8 will offer conclusions about the possible future of the regional integration process of the EU based on the analyses presented. For Europe and the world, the consequence of this process may be far-reaching both economically and politically.

NOTES

[1]*International Herald Tribune,* 28 March, 1996, pp. 1 and 6.

[2]*Financial Times,* 30 March, 1996, p. 2, and *London Times,* 27 March, 1996, p. 29. See also *Eurecom* 9, no. 1 (January 1997), p. 1.

2 THE EVOLUTION OF REGIONAL INTEGRATION THEORIES

When the European Coal and Steel Community (ECSC) was established in 1951 and began its operations in 1953, the question of a future United States of Europe was raised. The issue became more salient when the six original member states expanded their European activities by setting up the European Economic Community (EEC) and the European Atomic Energy Community (EURATOM) in 1957. These three organizations were seen as a possible basis for the economic and political unification of Europe, although the outcome was uncertain and to a large extent depended on the theoretical framework that might evolve from the activities of the three organizations.

Winston Churchill, in a speech in Zürich in 1948, seemed to advocate a united Europe, but he also recognized that an "Iron Curtain" had left the European continent, and with it Germany, divided in two.[1] The prospective members of the ECSC were anxious to have the United Kingdom join as a charter member, but Britain was not anxious to accept the proposal. It saw itself as operating within what Churchill described as three overlapping and interlocking relationships: the Empire and Commonwealth, the Atlantic Alliance, and the special relationship with the United States and Western Europe. Churchill emphasized that cessation of sovereignty—which integration implied—was neither desirable nor necessary. Although the EEC seemed to have much to offer, the problem set forth if Britain joined was its proposed supranationalism. This was perhaps the most important reason that Britain would not ever become an associate member of the ECSC, although economic changes in the Commonwealth and the general decline of British exports in the second half of the 1950s caused a change of view—despite the fact that the European Free Trade Association (EFTA), which included the Nordic countries, was set up in 1960. Meanwhile, Britain became anxious to join the EEC, but General deGaulle was opposed to British admission in 1963. It was in 1973 that the United Kingdom finally was admitted to the Community, along with Ireland and Denmark. The British desire to opt out of the Treaty of Maastricht during the various negotiations on the common currency and the social charter reflects both British attitudes and policies that remain inimical, to a large extent, to accepting political union. However, the new Labour government voted into power on May 1, 1997, may produce a change of attitude in the future.

Two basic theoretical strains could be identified in an expanding philosophical climate: 1) intergovernmentalism and 2) neo-functionalism. The first concept was based on interaction among national governmental institutions, when decisions were to be made for the operation of community activities and most of these decisions were made on a unanimous basis. The second concept originated in the assumptions developed originally by David Mitrany in his book, *A Working Peace System* (Chicago, 1966). These theories stressed both the creative work of solving common problems, and the habits of building Euro-national cooperation through which future constructive and beneficial collaboration was to replace the selfish quest for power as a dominant motive in international relations. Functionalism was seen as removing successive layers of sovereignty from the nation-states and eventually producing a world thoroughly oriented toward peace.

But will the integration process across national boundaries be more or less automatic and spread from economic sector to economic sector, thus enlarging the authority of international or regional institutions at the expense of national governments? This automaticity has been in doubt; consequently, in order to give functionalism a definite forward thrust in a particular region or set of issues, the school of neo-functionalism has advocated a number of strategies:

1. Regional institutions must be designed specifically to further the process of integration.
2. Politically significant social and economic sectors must be chosen to attain transnational collaboration, while according to Mitrany it was the *non*political sector that would have the best chances to promote integration.

3. The tasks given to regional institutions must be inherently expansive, culminating in "spill-over." This term refers to a situation created when the attainment of an original goal in the integration scheme can be achieved only by taking further action, which in turn may create additional situations requiring further action to attain regional goals.
4. Decisions must be made jointly by nation-states in a region, and the regional institutions must support the upgrading and advancement of the common interests of the region.
5. Technological experts serving the member governments must have political savvy, as well as skills to help with spill-over and to move the integration process forward.
6. Deliberate linkages between economic and political situations must be sought to ensure the full working of the expansive logic of sector integration.
7. The integration process may be aided by the formation of transnational groups and coalitions that perceive the upward movement of the process to be in their interest. Many of these groups are likely to consist of business elites whose shared goals and common interests in integration tend to assist in the adoption of regional values and aid in the socialization process.[2]

The applicability and value of neo-functionalism were seen as doubtful for the explanation of regional integration when Ernst Haas published "The Study of Regional Integration: Reflections on the Joy and Anguish of Pretheorizing" (*International Organization* 24, no. 3 (1970), pp. 631 ff.). But this did not end the theoretical concern with neo-functionalism as reflected by the work of Charles Pentland, *International Theory* (cited earlier, especially pp. 158–61).

Other bases for understanding regional integration are also valuable, although they are not as specific and comprehensive as the theoretical efforts discussed so far. One operates from a sociological foundation and focuses on the creation of a sense of community among individuals in the political units moving toward integration. Scholars prominent in this field are Karl W. Dentsch and Ronald Inglehart.[3]

Another theoretical approach is based on economic understanding of the community and economic integration generally. The best-known scholars are J. Viner and J. Bhagnati; details can be found in Alfred Tovias, "A Survey of the Theory of Economic Integration," in *European Integration*, edited by H. J. Michelmann and Panayotis Soldatos (New York, 1973, pp. 57–75).[4]

A final approach to institutional and decision-making systems for the EU is federalism, which would extol a clear-cut and effective relationship among the various heads of government while retaining the concept of state sovereignty among the participating units. It addresses itself to such issues as the division of power between component units and energizing central institutions. This can raise emotional opposition, as the people in the affected area are often reluctant to lose their national independence.

Federalism as an approach to European integration is centrally concerned with the creation of a federal governmental system, either through drafting an appropriate constitution by a convention of likely member states or by using the European Parliament as the basis for developing a federal system. The Single European Act (SEA) of 1987 and the Maastricht Treaty of 1993 can be seen as initial—but uncertain— stepping stones to a federal system, although the federal future is far from assured.[5]

After 1975, the quest for theorizing regarding the SEA and the problem of the Intergovernmental Conference at the beginning of the 1990s revived scholarly interest in the future of the EU regional integration process. Pursuing the intergovernmental route, Andrew Morarscik proposed a "liberal intergovernmentalist approach."[6] The claim of his article is that the EC can be analyzed as a successful intergovernmental regime designed to manage economic interdependence through negotiated policy coordination. This theory rests on the assumption that state behavior and objectives reflect the rational actions and goals of governments restrained at home by domestic societal processes and abroad by their strategic environment. An understanding of the preferences and powers of the member states is a logical starting point for analysis.[7]

The term used for the structure involved in the various decision-making processes is "international regime," whose content varies from place to place and task to task. Thus the term is not clear-cut but has the advantage of great flexibility, depending on the circumstances. Definitions of international regimes vary. According to Robert D. Keohane and Joseph S. Nye, they involve regulations and control of transnational and interstate relations by governments through the creation or acceptance of procedures, rules, and institutions for certain kinds of activity.[8] The most comprehensive concept of international regimes comes from Oran Young. He regards them as structures that may be more or less formally articulated and may or may not be accompanied by explicit organizational arrangements, although the core of every regime is seen by him as a collection of rights and rules. He also asserts that in formal terms "the members of an international regime are always sovereign states, although the parties carrying out the actions of government stipulated by international regimes are often private entities, for example, fishing companies or banks."[9]

Morarscik distinguishes three major activities in the management of member state economic interdependence through negotiated policy coordination. First, national preference formation must be considered. Groups of various compositions and concerns articulate preferences, and governments aggregate them. "The primary interest of governments is to maintain themselves in office; in democratic societies this requires the support of a coalition of domestic voters, parties, interest groups and bureaucracies, whose views are transmitted, directly or indirectly, through domestic institutions and promoters of political representation."[10] This is the basis of national preference formation, which underlies the struggle among EU member states to gain acceptance for their policy preferences in the integration process.

The negotiations among member states of the EU reflect not only the societal pressures and the expected magnitude of possible gains and losses, but also the interests of powerful groups in various countries. If these interests converge, they will make agreement within the EU easier, while divergence of interests may preclude any progress. The prospects for international agreement depend to a large extent on the configuration of societal preferences. EU member governments usually have little flexibility in making concessions or proposing linkages and, hence, may tend to settle on the lowest common denominator.

Finally, a few comments about the decision-making processes within the EU institutional framework. The basic rule over the last few decades has been that the Commission proposes and the Council of Ministers disposes. But this rule has been complicated by uncertainties about qualified voting procedures and the increasing impact of the rotating Council presidency as a key EU position. In general, some basic points need to be made. First, intergovernmental cooperation in the EU is voluntary; neither military coercion nor economic sanctions are threatened to force agreement. Most EU decisions, especially those of a significant nature, take place in a noncoercive unanimity voting system. Second, the environment in which EU member governments bargain is relatively information-rich; national governments send many of their experts to Brussels to participate in the discussions on specific problems, and they are well equipped to shed necessary light on the various problems under consideration and to examine the technical implications of policies that are of the greatest interest to the group.[11]

Third, the transaction costs of intergovernmental decision making are low. Negotiations within the EU take place over protracted periods of time, during which member governments can extend numerous offers and counteroffers at relatively little cost. Side-payments and linkages can be made. It is also possible to design various agencies to monitor and enforce any agreement at any desired level.[12]

If national governments are willing to accept only agreements that are closest to their preferred point, the range of possible agreements or solutions is very limited and lowest common denominator criteria are likely. Indeed, the trend toward unanimity decision making is strengthened and the EU's strong interest in effective policy making is undermined.[13]

Returning to the basics of neo-functionalism, the concept of "cooperative federalism" has emerged and been pursued by Simon Bulmer and Wolfgang Wessels,[14] as well as by Emil Kirchner.[15] The term advances interactions between EU institutions and various levels of state governments beyond specific allocations of power for decision making, to a model based on concurrent jurisdiction.[16] As time goes on, effective decision making in the EU may well require that a growing number of political objectives be achieved through ad hoc negotiations among federal states and perhaps even municipalities, which may strengthen favorable attitudes toward unanimity in solving problems, rather than toward qualified voting.

In setting the agenda for policy making in the EU, the Council presidency has assumed an increasing role and influence. It rotates every six months among the member states and is influential in the European Council, the Council of Ministers, the Committee of Permanent Representatives (COREPER, the French abbreviation of the body), and EU embassies in third countries. COREPER also organizes many working groups of national civil servants and thereby has considerable impact on setting the agenda of the EU.

The Council of Ministers meets in various compositions: First and foremost is the General Affairs Council, consisting of foreign ministers, which meets nearly every month and deals with European integration and foreign relations issues. A second type involves the Economic and Financial Council (ECOFIN) and the Agricultural Council. To assure coordination among the presidency and the various more specialized councils, a general secretariat of the Council of Ministers has been established. Three main features characterize this secretariat: a conference center, an administrative clearing house, and an advising body to the presidency. As time has passed, the secretary general has become an invaluable assistant to the council president in strengthening the operation of the EU top levels and increasing the effectiveness of the decision-making process.[17] As Hungary, Poland, and the Czech Republic may be the next countries to join the EU, the problems of the council presidency may become more difficult and EU decision making more complex. Hence, the secretariat's role in finding ways to accomplish an acceptable integration process will also be more crucial.

As a particular Council of Ministers converges to work on a decision in areas such as agriculture, or any other subject, the opposing arguments frequently give rise to controversial and long-lasting sessions. Success or failure of the process depends on various factors such as the agility and flexibility of the participants to devise and accept compromise formulae, the judgments of the Commission in this respect, the competence of the presidency, and the ability and willingness of the EU member governments to use majority voting. While the many meetings of national experts in the COREPER framework may seem to be favorable to evolving decisions even if the circumstances are complex, the Council meetings (which are held in secret) may last 24 hours or more and be characterized by an atmosphere of controversy and intense bargaining.[18] While these considerations affect the choice of the appropriate theory regarding the regional integration process in Europe, they also have an impact on the selection of what kind of democratic theory can be, or needs to be, applied to the evolution of the EU, and what its impact may be on the institutional and decision-making framework. This will be the topic of chapter 3.

NOTES

[1]Neill Nugent, *The Government and Politics of the European Community,* 2nd ed. (Durham, NC: Duke University Press, 1992), p. 16.

[2]An extensive literature exists on the various strands of the functionalist theory. The seminal work is Ernst R. Haas's *The Uniting of Europe* (Stanford, CA: Stanford University Press, 1955). Other important works are Leon N. Lindberg, *The Political Dynamics of European Economic Integration* (Stanford, CA: Stanford University Press, 1963) and Philip C. Schmitter "A Revised Theory of Regional Integration," *International Organization* 24, no. 4 (Autumn 1970), pp. 836–68. See also Haas "The Obsolescence of Regional Integration Theory," Research Series 25, *Institute of International Studies* (Berkeley, University of California, 1975).

[3]Karl W. Dentsch, *Political Community and the North Atlantic Area* (Princeton, NJ: Princeton University Press, 1957), p. 5; Ronald Inglehart, *The Silent Revolution* (Princeton, NJ: Princeton University Press, 1977), p. 4.

[4]Donald Puchala should also be mentioned here for his empirical studies on trade flows in the European Community. See "International Transactions and Regional Integration," *International Organization* 24 (1970), pp. 732–63.

[5]On the subject of federalism see also Charles Pentland, *International Theory and European Integration* (New York: The Free Press, 1973), pp. 158–61 and 166–74.

[6]Andrew Morarscik, "Preference and Power in the European Community: A Liberal Intergovernmentalist Approach," *Journal of Common Market Studies* 31, no. 4 (December 1993), pp. 473–519.

[7]Ibid., p. 474.

[8]Robert Keohane, *Power and Interdependence: World Politics in Transition* (Boston: Little, Brown, 1977), pp. 5–20.

[9]Oran R. Young. "International Regimes: Problems of Concept Formation," *World Politics* 32 (April 1980), pp. 31–56.

[10]Morascik, "Preference and Power," p. 483.

[11]Ibid., p. 498, and the references cited.

[12]Ibid.

[13]Ibid., also examples on pp. 500–2.

[14]European Commission, *The European Council: Decision-Making in European Politics* (London: Macmillan, 1987).

[15]Emil Kirchner, *Decision Making in the European Community* (Manchester and New York: Manchester University Press, 1992).

[16]Ibid., p. 11.

[17]For details see Ibid., pp. 72–87.

[18]A detailed description and analysis of Council meetings are found in Neill Nugent, *The Government and Politics of the European Community*, 2nd ed (Durham, NC: Duke University Press, 1991), pp. 100–28.

3 THE THEORY OF DEMOCRACY AND ITS INFLUENCE ON EU INTEGRATION

A complaint frequently heard among supporters of the European Union inside and outside its institutions concerns the existence of a "democratic deficit." It refers to a lack of majority voting in the decision-making process in the Council of Ministers, and it deplores the limited power of the European Parliament. On the other hand, the national parliaments of the EU member states and the regional parliaments in the federal system of Germany retain their political influence through their executive agencies, and there remains a strong tendency *against* offering democratic power directly to the EU institutions.

A paper by Dimitris N. Chryssochoou presented to the May 1995 ECSA Conference at Charleston, SC, has some interesting thoughts about the essential principles of representative democracy that may shape the realization between the collectivity (EU) and the segments (states). To accomplish this, transparency and decisional openness in the process of European decision making is essential. Other necessities are collective ministerial responsibility to the directly elected representatives of EU citizens, and the continuous and extensive control over the setting of the integrative political agenda through a functional distribution of responsibilities between the national parliaments and the European Parliament.[1] Under these circumstances, institutional and political elites pursuing their particular interests, sometimes contrary to peoples' true objectives, would be directed to the latter goals; and under such circumstances, regional integration in the EU could make greater progress. It is noteworthy that the number of proposals for principal legislation to be undertaken by the Commission had declined from 185 in 1990 to 52 in 1995.[2] Indeed, the possibilities for parliaments to hold the Commission-Council structure to account in a democratic environment are steadily decreasing.

Chryssochoou asserts that the role of member parliaments has remained extremely marginal in comparison to those of national and EU executive agents, and he believes that the *scope* of regional decision making actually has been determined within the secretive confines of various ministerial meetings and administrative committees and subcommittees, activities that are likely to bring difficulties to representative democracy that may have to operate on a transnational basis.[3]

The peculiarities of the EU situation can be summed up in the notion of confederal consociation. Its confining characteristics are 1) a fair separation of the segments of the overall EU framework, 2) domination of a "cartel of elites," 3) proportional representation of the states to central decision-making facilities (proportionality), and 4) the existence of a qualified right of a mutual veto.[4] These peculiarities must be seen in connection with the continuing growth of lobbyism, not only on the state and regional levels, but also on the level of the European institutions, especially the Commission and, more surprisingly, the European Parliament, which currently is working on specific rules of behavior and required formalities of lobbyists. As explained earlier, the growing number of these individuals is seen as a source of strength for the EP, although most final decisions are made by the Council of Ministers and strongly influenced by the national governments, which remain the seats of power. Some of the *Länder* governments in Germany, as well as Scotland, for example, have representatives in Brussels and may also be seen as influencing the EU decision-making process.

To consider realistically the practice of democracy in EU decision-making processes, one needs to think of the European Union as primarily a collective management of separate, national sovereignties.[5] Applying to this description the term confederal consociation, we are looking at a distinct form of political interstate organization and a new integrative dynamic among independent but yet highly interdependent bodies politic that remain conscious of their distinctive identities, pose no fundamental threat at least in constitutional terms, and whose legal relationships are based on an international treaty whose signature itself may be seen as providing confirmation of their individual sovereignties. This also means that while democratic support for EU legislative and administrative actions is available indirectly through the governments of the member states, slow forward movement on EU plans and actions can be anticipated. Only if the directly elected EP were to become the ultimate body to represent the European interests, which could transcend *national* divisions and interests, could we speak of a truly federated European polity and federal policies. Only under these circumstances could we talk about the EP assuming popular control over the territorially motivated Council of Ministers, which would allow us to claim that the EP could exercise legislative authority similar to that of other federal chambers.[6]

The foregoing situation was reflected in the IGC in Florence, Italy. A document presented by Italy to the 15 EU members identified the principles and conditions for allowing an advance guard of states to cooperate more closely without being held back by dissenters. The presumption of common action should prevail.[7] France, Germany, and the Benelux countries were pushing the "advance guard" principle, but several countries, notably Spain, had reservations in case they were left behind by a hard core inside the EU. Great Britain's future remains uncertain at present; a national referendum is a possibility and the 1997 elections will have a major influence. In the meantime, the problem of British beef affected by mad cow disease remains essentially unsettled, although the ban on British beef exports is being lifted gradually, which has given the IGC in Florence a shot in the arm. But disputes on this issue continue, with Germany banning beef imports from the United Kingdom, and France becoming increasingly concerned about spreading mad cow disease.[8]

Although, as already pointed out, the IGC may continue over a period of more than twelve months and may come under three more presidencies—Ireland, the Netherlands, and Luxembourg[9]—the outcome will not meet the desire for an EU democratic order. As already mentioned, the results of the conference may well depend on the parliamentary elections in Great Britain and even, under a Labour government, on a referendum regarding continued British membership in the EU and acceptance of the EMU. True democratic control of the EU remains elusive and becomes conditional on the interests and actions in evidence in the national parliaments. Although the system is flexible enough to exhibit varying degrees of pluralism according to separate interests involved in the EU decision-making process, the outcome of the various claims by national and regional organizations may be determined and controlled by the members of the cartel of elites. Multiple loyalties are likely to develop slowly, and in due time such loyalties and cross-cutting memberships, interests, and affiliations may emerge that could eventually strengthen the democratic character in the EU system. An example of possible change is Italy: One of the new prime minister Prodis's current objectives is federation, which would give Italy's regions more independence and more budget resources of their own.[10] If such a development occurred, democracy in the EU might be enhanced, as the interests and preferences of regional populations would increase their influence and expand representation.

The IGC, not having made much progress in Florence, had a special meeting in Dublin in October 1996 to accelerate the development of a Maastricht 2 Treaty. A more powerful meeting was held by the Irish Council presidency in December 1996, also in Dublin. Most EU countries support an extension of majority voting to avoid paralysis in decision making in an enlarged EU. France and Germany are pushing the idea of "flexible integration" to allow some countries to cooperate more closely in specific areas without being held back by dissidents. The priorities of the IGC as identified in the negotiations in Dublin included European citizenship conditions, unemployment (more than 18 million people out of work), immigration, protection of the environment, the fight against drugs and international crime, a more effective external policy, and reform of EU institutions. The technical preparations for a common currency are also part of the necessary priorities.[11]

Members of the EP supported austerity measures to overcome unemployment and assure sustainable growth. Commission president Santer wanted to shift $2.1 billion of surplus funds into transportation networks as well as research and development. But the United Kingdom wanted these funds reimbursed to national treasuries, and other EU members appeared to be similarly minded.[12]

EU employer groups and union groupings were ready to discuss working hours and labor flexibility prior to the Florence meeting and therefore seemed to be willing to support the Maastricht 2 plans of the Commission. In return, Santer has launched a "pact of confidence" to help the economy in the EU, which is officially named the Stability and Growth Pact.

EU ORGANIZATION AND THE ESSENTIALS OF DEMOCRACY

Moving the EU in the direction of a truly democratic system incorporating the essential principles of representative democracy in the political arrangements that are to shape the relations between the collectivity (EU) and the segments (states) is likely to be a difficult task. It will require meaningful legislative representation of EU citizens in central decision making, decisional openness and transparency in the making of European legislation, collective ministerial responsibility to the directly elected representatives of EU citizens, and continuous democratic control over the development of political agents who are supportive of integration through a functional distribution of responsibilities between the national parliaments and the European Parliament (EP).[13]

According to Chrissochoou, if a more civil, participatory, and considered program of integration is ever to become a political reality in the EU, it must effectively link different domains of political authority. In order for the tale of democracy in the EU to have a happy ending, beyond a purely national level, it is essential that the emerging system of EU government and politics act as the constructive level for a plurality of identities to flourish within a structure of mutual toleration and accountability. This requires the existence of mutually reinforcing legislation structures in and through which a plurality of forces can democratically coexist with each other.[14]

Majority voting may be the most adequate means of reaching decisions, but despite the seeming progress made through the Single European Act (SEA) of 1987, the EU member governments have reserved the right to veto anything that affects their vital interests. It appears then that the SEA did not supersede, but only circumscribed, the Luxembourg Accord of 1966, which allowed the veto.[15] The results of the 1996–97 IGC may be more specific on this and will be discussed in chapter 8.

Consociational theory sees the state apparatus as being an umpire and the bureaucracy of the Commission, as well as of COREPER, as the force to move integration forward. The European Parliament also aids this endeavor, but in the final analysis it is the cartel of elites that may have the last word regarding the process and goals of the integration movement.[16] In the spring of 1996, the British government, never sure how much it should support the European institutions and regulations, began to become so upset about the ban on British beef exports imposed by the EU Commission that Prime Minister John Major said that Britain would use its veto to block the passage of all European Union initiatives requiring unaniminity. It would do all it could to disrupt European business, including obstructing the IGC and summit conferences in Florence, Dublin, Amsterdam, and Luxembourg until the European institutions eased the British beef ban.[17]

To expand democracy further within the EU, the Maastricht Treaty of 1993 permitted the establishment of a Committee of Regions, and through it increased the involvement of national parliaments in policy development. In addition, regular meetings take place between presidents or speakers of national parliaments. A conference of bodies specializing in

European affairs in the various assemblies of the EU (COSAC) meets regularly, but the Assizes—a conference of parliaments—has not been convened since one held in Rome in December 1990. Although the SEA has shifted additional decision-making powers to the EU institutions, the populations in different member states do not seem to have transferred their emotional nationalistic support for these states to the EU as a whole.[18] Part of the problem is the lack of transparency in the negotiations among the EU decision makers, and the uncertainty of citizens regarding how the EU decisions will affect them. This uncertainty, in turn, affects public opinion, which will be discussed in a later chapter. Meanwhile, the British government must realize that some topics to be decided in the Council of Ministers can be done by qualified majority vote. But the list of provisions that authorize qualified majority vote is not very large and does not include the more sensitive subjects.[19] It follows that the scope of regional decision making has remained largely within the secretive confines of various ministerial meetings, administrative committees, and subcommittees, with a very minor role taken by member parliaments, thus providing a difficult situation for representative democracy for the region as a whole.[20]

Use of the term *Gesellschaft* for the current system established by the Maastricht Treaty, which makes the EU institutions cooperating actors in policy making with the national and regional governments, could be considered as a possible step toward a *Gemeinschaft*, which would extend people-based democracy to the operations of the EU institutions. Perhaps the realization of the idea of a "Europe of regions" as opposed to the notion of a "Europe of states," but also recognizing the principle of "government by elite cartel," may create strong popular demand for an immediate and substantive increase in the democratic properties of the central political system.[21] This, then, would reflect the characteristics of *Gemeinschaft* as a much closer relationship among people living in a particular territory and would give added strength to the EU as a viable political organization.

Since June of 1996, when the Italian presidency of IGC came to an end and Ireland took over, the Commission has continued to look for EU progress in the following areas:

- The Union must act democratically, transparently, and in a way people can understand;
- The Union must act "effectively, consistently, and in solidarity," in both its internal workings and its external relations, to emphasize a genuine European identity. The prospect of the Union's expansion to 20 or more member states underscores this necessity.

One of the current Maastricht Treaty's objectives in terms of democracy is the concept of European citizenship. This will not replace national citizenship, but is designed to give members of the EU countries a feeling of belonging to a larger unit as well.

Finally, democratic legitimacy in the EU is enhanced by making the appointment of the Commission members subject to the approval of the EP. The legislative powers of the EP have been expanded, especially through the Single European Act, and it is possible that the IGC may add to the enlargement of democracy.[22] At the same time, the Commission reports the "systematic recourse to unanimity in various decision-making undertakings, including especially in the field of foreign policy."[23] The Commission hopes for a radical overhaul of the decision-making arrangements as well as a review of the feasibility of different speeds of integration, but is utterly opposed to a Europe "a la carte," which in its opinion "would lead inevitably to a negation of Europe."[24]

One small step forward toward democracy in the EU is the cooperation procedure introduced by the SEA. It involves a complex system of interactions among the European Parliament, the Council of Ministers, and the Commission, and has enjoyed at least a limited success in the adoption of proposed EP amendments by the Council of Ministers.[25]

LOBBYING IN THE EU

In a democratic system, the formation of policy preferences may arise from various sources and on multiple levels; this is especially the case in a complex institutional organization such as the European Union. Lobbying by various interest groups can be a powerful tool to transform group objectives into policies endorsed by either national or union agencies, and influences by these groups may also be exerted on the local or intermediate level such as the *Länder* in Germany. However, interest group activity influencing governmental outcomes may undermine the ideal operation of democracy—which is based on majority voting and detailed constitutional instructions for the implementation of laws, regardless of the economic and political power of intervening groups.

According to Mazey and Richardson, European-wide interest group federations have existed since the early days of the European Communities in industries such as agriculture, coal, and steel. By 1970 more than 300 Euro-groups existed, and in 1992 the number of Euro-groups formally recognized by the Commission had risen to over 500.[26] The Commission is the primary target of much of European lobbying, but the European Parliament, despite its relative lack of power, also has been concerned by these activities for a number of reasons, not the least of which is the very intrusive behavior of some lobbyists in the EP buildings in Brussels and in Strassburg. Indeed, it may well be that the number of lobbyists has been increased further: some estimates go as high as 3,000, and as regards the EP, one important reason is the Single European Act, which has increased the influence of the EP.[27] There is much discussion about a code of conduct for the lobbyists. It would require them to sign a public register and, while on the premises of the Parliament, to wear a named pass or badge at all times. It would also make it compulsory for lobby groups to produce an annual declaration listing all favors, gifts, and acts of generosity of any nature, valued over a certain sum (ECU 1000), that have been provided to members of the EP, civic servants, and European Parliament assistants. Members of the EP also were called upon to make a declaration at the start and at the end of every parliamentary term of any donations, gifts, or other paid activities. Such declarations are to be updated every year in a register open to the public. These important transparency measures so far have not been accepted by the majority of the EP membership.

Who are the lobbyists? There are about 140 professional public affairs consultants, 160 law firms, and more than 500 trade associations based in Brussels. To these can be added the Brussels offices of 200 major multinational firms, and diplomats from all parts of the world, as well as representatives of some regional and local authorities. Despite the increase in the number of lobbyists in the European Parliament and the Commission, it should be emphasized that maximum power continues to reside in the EU members' governments, and qualified majority voting requires 70 percent of the votes in order to have a proposal accepted as law.[28]

As Nugent points out, decision making in the EU Council usually proceeds on the understanding that difficult and controversial items are *not* proposed. Where it is clear that a state or states have serious difficulties with a proposal, they are normally allowed time. Usually, the controversial item is held over for a further meeting, with the hope that, in the meantime, informal meetings or perhaps COREPER will be the basis for a solution.[29] Such a situation, of course, may also induce lobbyists in various institutions to exert their efforts to find solutions for the proposal, as a result of which their involvement can be very useful in specific instances.

As the EP assumes greater power, the interests of lobbyists are bound to increase. Two groups can be identified: representatives of business and single-interest groups. Those lobbyists representing powerful business interests watch legislative proposals very carefully and seek to persuade MEPs to back amendments that would weaken the impact of any legislation with a potentially adverse impact on the industries they represent. The motor industry is a case in point, as it anxiously follows moves to tighten pollution. Another instance is the vote on a Commission proposal for a European-wide ban on tobacco advertising, which may be opposed by a blocking minority of national governments when the issue comes to a vote in the Council of Ministers. Second, there are single-issue pressure groups, often voluntary organizations, seeking EP support for a particular cause. An example is Greenpeace, which maintains close links with the party of the Greens in the EP.

THE IMPACT ON PUBLIC OPINION

Considering that lobbying has become one of Europe's growth industries, it is reasonable to assume that, on specific issues, the objectives pushed by powerful groups and associations may pervade public opinion. In turn, favorable public opinion may be essential for policy developments supporting both a closer, democratic relationship in the European Union as well as interactions among the growing number of member states.

Since 1973 public opinion surveys have been conducted twice a year by the Commission in member states through the Directorate-General for Information, Communication, Culture, and Audio Visual of the European Commission, and have been expanded as the EU membership increased to the present number of 15. The basic number of interviewees is 1000 per member state, but the number was reduced to 500 for Luxembourg and enlarged to 2000 for Germany (West and East). The publication of the results is carried out in the *Eurobarometer* every six months; since 1990 a publication called *Eurobarometer Trends* has also been available, and some of the trend data may be useful later for our analysis.

Public opinion can, of course, also be expressed by referenda on specific issues within an EU member state. Examples are a 1972 referendum in France to ratify the enlargement of the Community, referenda during the same year in Denmark and Ireland to become EU members, and a referendum in 1975 in the United Kingdom on continued Community membership. In 1986 Denmark held a referendum on the ratification of the SEA, and in 1987 Ireland did the same. In 1989 a referendum was carried out in Italy on the question of whether the European Community "should be transformed into an effective Union." In all these referenda, majority votes were cast for the pro-Community side of the question. [30]

Referenda were also held in Denmark and France regarding the acceptance of the Maastricht Treaty on European Union, which finally entered into force on November 1, 1993. The majorities in these referenda were small, but they were sufficient to have the contents of the Treaty go forward. However, in an initial referendum in Denmark on the Maastricht Treaty in 1992, the outcome was negative.

Election to the EP every five years could also be seen as an expression of public opinion, but it should be emphasized that, since the elections are not contested by European parties standing on European issues but are more second-order national elections, they can hardly be regarded as reflections of the European policy preferences of the populace.[31] A detailed analysis of the *Eurobarometer* findings (1996) will be presented in chapter 6.

NOTES

[1]Dimitris Chryssochoou, Paper presented at the ECSA Conference, Charleston, SC, May 1995, p. 2.

[2]Commission Report, *Intergovernmental Conference 1996*, p. 85.

[3]Chryssochoou, Paper presented at the ECSA Conference, Charleston, SC, May 1995, pp. 5–6.

[4]For a detailed discussion of these concepts see Paul Taylor, "Consocialionalism and Federalism as Approaches to International Integration," in *Frameworks for International Cooperation*, eds. A. J. R. Groom and Paul Taylor (New York: St. Martin's Press, 1990), pp. 172–84.

[5]See A. J. R. Groom, "The European Commonality Building Up, Breaking Down, and Building Across," *Conference Proceedings, People's Rights and European Structures*. Centro Unesco de Catalunya, 1993.

[6]See Chryssochoou, paper presented at the ECSA Conference, Charleston, SC, May 1995, p. 10.

[7]*Financial Times,* 18 June, 1996, p. 2.

[8]*Denver Post,* 20 June, 1996, p. 15A. See also *Financial Times,* 8–9 March, 1997, p. 1.

[9]Incoming EU states are kept informed through the so-called troika system.

[10]*New York Times*, 21 June, 1996, p. A19.

[11]*Financial Times*, 22–23 June, 1996. See also *Eurecom*, January 1997, p. 1.

[12]Ibid.

[13]Ibid.

[14]Ibid. pp. 2–3.

[15]This is the view of Paul Taylor in "Consocialionalism and Federalism as Approaches to International Integration," in *Frameworks for International Cooperation*, eds. A. J. R. Groom and Paul Taylor (New York: St. Martin's Press, 1990), pp. 172–84.

[16]For additional analysis, see ibid.

[17]*New York Times*, 24 May, 1996, p. A4.

[18]Interviews in Belgium and Italy during 1995 and 1996. See also the *Eurobarometer* data in chapter 5.

[19]See the Commission Report for the Reflection Group, Annex 8, *Intergovernmental Conference 1996*, pp. 80–85.

[20]See Chryssochoou, Paper presented at the ECSA Conference, Charleston, SC, May 1995, pp. 5–11.

[21]Ibid., p. 23.

[22]See the Commission Report for the Reflection Group, p. 6.

[23]Ibid., p. 7.

[24]Ibid., p. 8.

[25]For a detailed discussion of the Cooperation Procedure see Neill Nugent, *The Government and Politics of the European Community*, 2nd ed. (Durham, NC: Duke University Press, 1991), pp. 291–98.

[26]Sonia Mazey and Jeremy Richardson, "Pressure Groups and Lobbying in the EC," in *The European Community and the Challenge of the Future*, 2nd ed., ed. Juliet Lodge (New York: St. Martin's Press, 1993), pp. 37–47.

[27]Interview with several EP members in October 1995 and January 1996.

[28]Under the qualified majority voting rules France, Germany, the U.K., and Italy have ten votes each. Spain has eight. Belgium, Greece, the Netherlands, and Portugal have five; Austria and Sweden four; and Denmark and Finland three.

[29]Nugent, *Government and Politics*, p. 122.

[30]Ibid., pp. 374–75.

[31]Ibid., p. 375.

4 THE ECONOMIC OUTLOOK IN THE EU AND ITS IMPACT ON THE PROGRESS OF POLITICAL DEVELOPMENT

While favorable public opinion is an essential ingredient for the continuing integration of the EU, the development of such opinion requires strong, positive economic conditions in the region characterized by continuing increases in employment and a stable financial underpinning. This means that fiscal deficits should be avoided or held to a minimum. Gross Domestic Product (GDP) growth should be maintained, hopefully at a reasonable level, thus assuring that fiscal deficits will be either nonexistent or fairly small.

In May of 1996 the European Commission unveiled its projections for that year and for 1997, both of which are found in Table 4-1. Despite the fact that the data are disappointing, especially for 1996, improvements can be seen for 1997 if the projections are accurate, indicating a more optimistic future.

The importance of these data is related to the Maastricht Treaty's conditions that must be met by EU member states in order to participate in the common currency (see Articles 109h to 109m, *Maastricht Treaty on European Union*). These provisions focus on excessive budget deficits in the member states and deal in great detail with the ramifications and consequences of such deficits, as well as the necessary corrections to assure the proper operation of the common currency by the EU states that have been found acceptable as EMU members. Due provision is that for EU members to become participants in the common currency, the GDP deficit gap must not exceed 3 percent in 1997. This will allow them to be members of the system in 1999. Under current circumstances, it appears doubtful whether even Germany and France may qualify,[1] although both countries want to be charter members of the common currency and will likely be successful in their efforts.

As GDP deficits are linked at times to the pay demands of powerful labor unions, the Commission has made efforts to persuade the unions to tie these demands to the broader goal of the common currency, which could suffer if unemployment remains high as the result of labor contract nonacceptance by unions—which in some countries such as Germany and France are very powerful.[2]

Table 4-1 shows that estimated GDP growth for the EU as a whole will move from 2.6 percent in 1996 to 2.9 percent in 1997. The latest information of the European Commission *(1997 Annual Economic Report Regarding Growth, Employment, and Convergence on the Road to EMU)* shows that, provided current spending plans for 1997 are adhered to, budgeting consolidation in that year is expected to be achieved mainly through expenditure restraint. Thus until the year 1998, the Community is expected to achieve a significant reduction in the share of public expenditures in GDP of around 2.5 percentage points, while tax pressure is forecast to remain broadly unchanged (see Table 4-2). These figures indicate progress with respect to the initiation of the common currency. Luxembourg is the only country suffering no fiscal deficit in both years; the highest deficit countries are Greece, 6.9 percent, and Portugal and Belgium, both with a 3.7 percent deficit.

All this injects a measure of uncertainty about the future of the common currency in the EU. Most of the member states, even Germany and France, may have to increase their taxes or institute cuts in governmental personnel—moves that may unfavorably affect public opinion, support for the EU that is needed for strengthening effective decision making in the institutional framework of the Community.

The degree of unemployment also plays an important role in this connection. From 1973, when the unemployment rate in the Community of the Six was 2.4 percent, to 1996, with a rate of nearly 12 percent, the number of unemployed has nearly quadrupled in the EU. In some of the member states, including France, the percentage increases were even higher (12.3 percent).[3] But projections to the year 2000 regarding German deficits and for the Maastricht Treaty criteria are favorable. According to Table 4-1, in 1997 the government's deficit as a percentage of GDP will already be reduced to 2.9 percent, and by the year 2000 it is expected to have fallen to 1.5 percent, although in net figures total public spending and total revenues will have continued to rise. This may indicate that by the year 2000 public opinion may be in support of EU, as unemployment is likely to fall and economic conditions to improve. By that time, also, the British beef issue is likely to be resolved, and the United Kingdom may either show new incentives within the EU framework or have completely withdrawn, although against the wishes of many British corporations.[4]

The French government, facing a GDP deficit of 4.2 percent in 1996, is anticipating a reduction of this deficit to 3 percent in 1997 and thus would qualify for becoming a common currency member in that year. This also means that former French prime minister Alan Juppés's financial plans, often a target of serious criticism, especially by the unions in France, have been modified by the Socialist Jospin government and have found broader support by the population in general.[5]

In order to provide more detailed data on key economic factors in the EU, I have included some tables and charts dealing with the number of unemployed in the EU, the GDP, and inflation. The data include forecasts of the Commission for 1996 and 1997 (Table 4-1) and details on employment and compensation (Tables 4-3, 4-4, 4-5, 4-6, 4-7). According to the data presented, EU growth and employment lagged; GDP may have increased only 2.6 percent in 1996 but grew in 1997 by 2.9 percent. The employment situation is even more worrying: unemployment will decline only to about 10.5 percent at the end of 1997 after holding at nearly 11 percent in 1996. On the other hand, inflation remains in check. Eleven EU member states have met the inflation criterion in 1995, and inflation is likely to decline further in 1997. Government borrowing has also gone down and is estimated to follow this trend in 1996 and 1997. The figure was 6.2 percent in 1993 and is expected to be -3.4 percent in 1997. What are the reasons for this downward trend? The Commission believes that the effects of monetary turbulence in the spring of 1995 were greater than anticipated and the long-term interest rates in 1994 and 1995 were too high.[6] But it is certain that economic convergence is moving forward and that introduction of the single currency on January 1, 1999, remains a realistic assumption. The projection for 1997 is that seven EU member states (Denmark, Germany, France, Ireland, Luxembourg, the Netherlands, and Finland) would have deficits below 3 percent, and six others (Austria, Sweden, Belgium, Spain, Portugal, and the United Kingdom) would have deficits between 3 and 3.7 percent.[7]

As already mentioned, both the forecasts for 1996 and the scenario for 1997 are based on the assumption of unchanged economic policies. While most EU member states had adopted their budget laws for 1996, the scenario for 1997 shows a likely outcome, if no further budget policy measures were to be taken.[8]

Another problem that may be upsetting the forecasts could be the EU's ban on British beef exports (to stop the so-called "mad cow disease"), which the U.K. government has sought to overcome by a policy of non-cooperation with other members of the union. Although some progress was made in June 1996, to overcome the British policy, the president of the Commission, Jacques Santer, insisted that the United Kingdom must not jeopardize the decision-making process of the EU and requested the elimination of the conflictual British policy.[9] But only a very small number of Commission and Council of Ministers proposals received British consent when unanimity was required, and the number of proposals needing qualified voting approval was small.

The labor market may enjoy moderate improvement in the years ending the twentieth century, after employment had fallen by more than 6 million over the period 1992–94. It rose by about 0.75 percent in 1995 and was expected to grow about 1 percent in 1996 through the creation of 2.4 million jobs over the next two years. The rise in employment is aided by wage restraint, as the growth of real wages was less than 1 percent below productivity growth in 1995. Better job prospects to induce a return to the labor market by discouraged workers, and a higher number of new job seekers, could lead to renewed growth in the labor force in 1996–97. However, given the continued high level of unemployment, labor discouragement is expected to subside only gradually, and the growth of the labor force should remain somewhat below the level registered during the boom years 1986–90. The favored countries for the reduction of unemployment up to 1997 are expected to be Denmark, Spain, Ireland, and Finland.[10]

The unemployment factor has a considerable impact on public opinion, as mentioned earlier, and I will discuss in detail in the next chapter the support of the EU population for the progress of integration. At the same time, unemployment is likely to negatively affect domestic government positions in the EU member states—a good example of which is France and the concerns expressed by both President Chirac and former Prime Minister Juppés about their relations with powerful French labor unions.[11]

FOREIGN ECONOMIC DEVELOPMENT

To obtain a greater insight into the integration potential of the EU, it is useful to look carefully at the foreign economic developments of the 15 member states. Table 4-8 provides comparative information on the export of goods, specifically on the percentage changes of volume from 1974 to 1997. With respect to the European Union there has been a steady increase in volume, for which the increase in the number of member states from 1974 to 1997 is, in part, responsible. But while some decline of exports of member states can also be noted, especially in 1993, the overall picture regarding individual export volume is encouraging for the EU and its members.

The world trade balance enjoyed by the EU is also favorable, as can be seen from Table 4-9. Indeed, the EU has the highest favorable balance (estimated) in 1996 and 1997, with the United States having the highest projected deficits in these years.

The position of the EU in the international economic environment is depicted in Table 4-10 and shows the Union with a very moderate (2.9 percent) increase estimated for 1997. This is above the United States and Japan (3.2 percent and 2.9 percent respectively) but below the central European countries, which now have association agreements with the EU, and the former Soviet Union (8.5 percent), as well as the so-called Dynamic Asian Economies (DAE) at 7.3 percent. The growth of extra-EC export markets appears to be moderating and is estimated to be 8.4 percent in 1997. It may continue to deteriorate slightly but will remain an important aspect of the EU economy.

The foreign economic data regarding the EU may strengthen supports for the institutional objectives but, at least for 1997, they are informed projections and may not be fully realized. The proceedings at the IGC in Florence were not encouraging; they were under Ireland's presidency when the next conference took place in October and December in Dublin.[12] In the meantime, a plan to put some of Europe's 18 million unemployed to work—with a $1.5 billion public works package to be dedicated to transcontinental road and rail projects—was delayed for more study by Britain, Germany, and the Netherlands. However, a compromise was reached on a pan-European police unit—Europol—that, however, exempts Britain from key provisions. The average budget deficit is estimated to decline to 4.7 percent of GDP and, considering unchanged fiscal policies, is projected to fall to about 3 percent of GDP in 1997.

SOCIAL FACTORS

The support of social conscience in the exercise of economic pursuits has always been a desirable goal in the expanding European Community. This is affirmed in the Maastricht Treaty (Articles 130a and b). The progress that can be made to achieve social and economic cohesion is considered to be a high-priority EU target, although optional exclusions exist for member states and have been taken by Great Britain.

Two main concerns of the EU in the social area since the late 1980s have been adoption of the Community Charter of Fundamental Social Rights for Workers and the establishment of a European Social Fund. The Charter contained a number of themes, including the free movement of workers on the basis of equal treatment in access to employment and social protection; employment on the basis of "fair remuneration"; improvement of living and working conditions; freedom of association and collective bargaining; and protection of children and adolescents. The Commission, at the end of December 1989, drew up an action program on the application of the Charter emphasizing the social divisions of the internal market and addressing the national and community responsibilities in this matter.[13]

The European Social Fund is primarily concerned with vocational training and employment promotion activities, especially among youth; it is part of the voluntary annual EU budget expenditures and receives about 8 percent of the budget. This is less than is received by the European Regional Development Fund (ERDF), which obtains 11 percent and whose aim is the correction of serious disparities in levels of development and prosperity in difficult regions of the EU.[14]

It is likely that, because of the high priority enjoyed by the social concerns in most of the member states, the application of the pertinent funds will continue after EU enlargement into Eastern Europe. But the variety of the income levels in the prospective member countries may introduce new priorities for these funds, which may change their principles and operations. In a broader sense, enlargement, especially into Eastern Europe, will raise important questions for the EU. How can the members enhance their capacity to take decisions and to act when their diversity becomes more pronounced? We have to be aware of the implications of the EU for the institutions and policies of the Union. The Commission is convinced that there are answers to these questions. It asserts that "there is no compelling reason why an endeavor based on openness and solidarity should mean weakness and dilution: enlargements and deepening are perfectly compatible."[15] But the outcome of the Florence, Italy, meeting showing a minimum of accomplishments on the various conference items, was not persuasive of future success and is indicative of continuing problems.

It is anticipated that the first East European countries will join the EU between 2002 and 2007. Malta and Cyprus may be able to become members earlier, depending on the settlement of the Greek-Turkish dispute over Cyprus.[16] But there are questions about the impact of the expansion on the EU budget; the cost for the EU may be high, and some shifting of funds may be necessary—such as selected reductions of the regional aid fund and their shift to East European countries, perhaps already ahead of accession. Other countries—France, Belgium, and the Netherlands—may no longer qualify for EU aid. Nevertheless, the Commission believes that the cost of adding East European countries will burden the EU budget only minimally.[17]

Another problem of the future is the British attitude toward the EU social concerns, as developed under former Prime Minister John Major. The British opted out of the EU Social Charter endeavor, and this split between Britain and the other EU members has become increasingly wider. This division is at least partially because Major wanted to force the remainder of the EU members to halt the beef boycott, but also to show his opposition to many items that are to be discussed in the Maastricht IGC, such as increased majority voting and the EMU progress. This has caused an increasingly negative stand by other EU members against Britain, strengthened by a vituperous campaign on the part of various British tabloids against the EU and, especially, Germany.[18] Unless British attitudes change radically, the loss of its EU membership may be a question not of London's withdrawal but of being pushed out by unhappy EU national governments and the Commission. However, all this may change with the assumption of the prime minister's position by Labour leader Tony Blair.

At the same time, Germany, a long-time stalwart of maintaining social concerns, has begun to approve welfare cuts aiming at a reduction of $16.5 billion from federal spending next year, amid claims by the social-democratic opposition that this step would destroy Germany's social foundation.[19]

Attachment to the Community's social policy generally has been strong except in the United Kingdom. Jacques Delors, the former Commission president, insisted on a "social Europe" to support the achievements of the single market for goods and services. If this market is to work effectively, the European workforce must be considered as integrated and mobile, implying common conditions of employment, central recognition of qualifications, and equal benefits for workers and their families.[20]

The social protocol attached to the Maastricht Treaty contains significant additions to the policy-making structure of the EU. It introduces the principle of subsidiarity—which is complex, as it prohibits final action by EU institutions on an issue unless the EU has the only means to achieve objectives of the Treaty and the problem cannot be tackled by the appropriate and affected member state or a still lower level of government. Therefore, in some instances, "subsidiarity" may impair appropriate action under the protocol and reduce the possibility for a desirable social policy.[21]

What emerges from the discussion in this chapter is the variety of economic and social factors influencing the program of the integration of the EU area, as well as the continuing struggles affecting EU policy making and the application of democratic principles.[22] One of the economic and social concerns discussed and fought over is the possibility of a common currency for all EU countries, an event that could become the touchstone of regional integration. A broad discussion of this topic will be presented in the next chapter.

NOTES

[1]*Financial Times,* 16 May, 1996, p. 2.

[2]*Financial Times,* 15 May, 1996, p. 1.

[3]See David R. Carmeron, "The 1992 Initiative: Causes and Consequences," in *Euro-Politics,* ed. Alberta M. Sbragia (Washington, DC: The Brookings Institution, 1991), pp. 23–74.

[4]See various articles in the *Financial Times,* 10 June, 1996, pp. 1, 2, 5.

[5]*Financial Times,* 11 June, 1996, p. 3. See also Table 4-2.

[6]*European Union News,* 15 May, 1996, no. 30/96. The spring 1996 Commission forecasts are found in Table 1-4.

[7]Ibid. and Tables 4-1 and 4-2.

[8]European Commission, *European Economy,* Supplement A, Economic Trends, no. 12, December 1995.

[9]*New York Times,* 6 June, 1996, p. A6.

[10]*European Economy,* Supplement A, and Table 4-16 for EU.

[11]*Financial Times,* 15 May, 1996, p. 1.

[12]*Colorado Springs Gazette Telegraph,* 23 July, 1996, p. A14.

[13]For details see Neill Nugent, *The Government and Politics of the European Community* (Durham, NC: Duke University Press, 1991) p. 258.

[14]Ibid., p. 320. It should be noted that the U.K. participates in the ERDF.

[15]The Commission Report for the Reflection Group, Annex 8, *Intergovernmental Conference 1996,* p. 4.

[16]*Financial Times,* 26 June, 1996, p. 1.

[17]Ibid.

[18]See the excellent analysis by Ian Davidson, *Financial Times,* 26 June, 1996, p. 12.

[19]*Denver Post,* 29 June, 1996, p. 9A.

[20]Edward Moxon-Browne, "Social Europe," in *The European Community and the Challenge of the Future,* ed. Juliet Lodge (New York: St. Martin's Press, 1993), pp. 152–62.

[21]Ibid., p. 164.

[22]The introduction of work week regulations opposed by the U.K. continues to move forward and has caused substantial legal problems, despite the British "opt-out." See details in the *Financial Times,* 27 June, 1996, p. 13.

TABLE 4-1: Gross Domestic Product, Volume (Percentage Change, at Constant Prices, on Preceding Year, 1961–97)

	1961-73	1974-85	1986-90	1991-93	1994-97	1991	1992	1993	1994	1995	1996	1997*
B	4.9	1.8	3.0	0.8	2.3	2.2	1.8	-1.6	2.2	2.3	2.2	2.6
DK	4.3	2.0	1.4	1.2	3.4	1.3	0.8	1.5	4.4	3.4	2.6	3.2
D	4.3	1.7	3.4	2.0	2.6	5.0	2.2	-1.2	2.9	2.1	2.4	3.1
GR	7.7	2.5	1.7	1.1	1.8	3.2	0.8	-0.5	1.5	1.7	1.9	2.2
E	7.2	1.9	4.5	0.6	2.8	2.2	0.7	-1.1	2.0	3.0	2.9	3.2
F	5.4	2.2	3.2	0.2	2.7	0.8	1.3	-1.5	2.7	2.8	2.4	2.8
IRL	4.4	3.8	4.6	3.1	6.0	2.2	3.9	3.1	6.7	6.7	5.6	4.8
I	5.3	2.8	3.0	0.2	2.8	1.2	0.7	-1.2	2.2	3.2	3.0	2.9
L	4.0	1.8	4.6	1.7	3.6	3.1	1.9	0.3	4.4	3.1	3.3	3.5
NL	4.8	1.8	3.1	1.5	2.7	2.3	2.0	0.2	2.7	3.0	2.5	2.8
A	4.9	2.2	3.0	1.6	2.7	2.9	1.8	-0.1	3.0	2.4	2.5	2.8
P	6.9	2.2	5.1	0.7	2.5	2.1	1.1	-1.2	1.1	2.7	3.1	3.3
FIN	5.0	2.7	3.4	-4.0	4.3	-7.1	-3.6	-1.2	4.0	4.8	4.4	4.1
S	4.1	1.8	2.3	-1.7	2.8	-1.1	-1.4	-2.6	2.2	3.7	2.6	2.5
UK	3.1	1.4	3.3	-0.2	3.0	-2.0	-0.5	2.0	3.8	2.6	2.7	2.7
EUR	4.8	2.0	3.3	0.6	2.8	1.5	1.0	-0.6	2.8	2.7	2.6	2.9
USA	3.9	2.3	2.8	1.8	3.2	-0.5	2.5	3.4	4.1	3.2	2.3	3.2
JAP	9.6	3.6	4.5	1.7	1.4	4.3	1.1	-0.2	0.5	0.4	2.3	2.6

*Projections.

Source: European Commission services.

TABLE 4-2: General Government Receipts and Expenditures (Percent of GDP)

	Receipts				Expenditures			
	1995	1996	1997*	1998*	1995	1996	1997*	1998*
B	50.3	50.5	50.1	49.7	54.5	53.8	53.0	52.1
DK	58.1	58.8	58.0	56.4	59.7	60.3	58.2	56.7
D	46.3	45.7	46.0	45.9	49.9	49.7	48.9	48.2
GR	37.6	38.0	38.4	38.7	46.7	46.0	44.9	44.0
E	39.7	40.3	40.5	40.2	46.3	44.8	43.5	43.0
F	49.5	50.6	50.5	50.2	54.3	54.7	53.5	53.1
IRL	35.4	34.7	34.3	33.9	37.4	36.3	35.2	34.3
I	44.8	46.3	47.7	47.1	51.8	52.9	51.0	50.1
L	40.8	41.7	41.2	40.8	40.0	40.7	40.7	39.9
NL	49.1	48.3	47.7	47.0	53.2	50.9	50.1	49.0
A	46.9	48.2	48.7	48.3	52.8	52.5	51.7	51.2
P	40.1	40.4	41.3	41.1	45.3	44.5	44.3	44.0
FIN	53.5	55.3	54.3	53.9	58.8	58.7	56.5	55.3
S	60.1	63.0	61.7	60.5	68.2	66.9	64.6	61.5
UK	37.8	37.6	37.7	38.0	43.5	42.3	41.3	40.2
EUR	**45.8**	**46.2**	**46.4**	**46.1**	**50.9**	**50.6**	**49.4**	**48.5**

*Projections.

Source: European Commission services.

	1960	1973	1985	1990	1991[1]	1991[2]	1995
1. Population in working age group (15-64 years)*	193.8	208.4	229.7	234.2	235.4	246.0	249.0
2. Activity rate in % (= 3 / 1)	68.9	66.9	65.7	67.2	67.3	67.7	66.6
3. Active population (= 4 + 5)*	133.4	139.5	150.9	157.5	158.3	166.6	165.9
4. Unemployment*	3.1	3.5	14.8	12.0	12.7	13.6	17.9
5. Total employment*	130.4	136.0	136.2	145.4	145.6	153.0	148.1
6. Employment rate (= 5 / 1)*	67.3	65.2	59.3	62.1	61.9	62.2	59.5
7. Potential employment at 1961-73 average employment rate (66.2%)*	128.4	138.1	152.2	155.2	155.9	163.0	165.0
8. Employment gap 1 (= 5 - 7)*	2.0	-2.1	-16.0	-9.7	-10.3	-10.0	-16.9
9. Potential employment at 70% employment rate[3],*	135.6	145.9	160.8	163.9	164.8	172.2	174.3
10. Employment gap 2 (= 5 - 9)*	-5.3	-10.0	-24.6	-18.5	-19.1	-19.3	-26.2

* In millions.

[1] 1960–91 with West Germany.

[2] 1991–95 with unified Germany.

[3] Comparable to highest employment rates registered in Northern Europe, USA, and Japan.

Source: European Commission services.

TABLE 4-4: Compensation of Employees Per Head (Percentage Change on Preceding Year, 1961–97)

	1961-73	1974-85	1986-90	1991-93	1994-97	1991	1992	1993	1994	1995	1996	1997*
B	9.0	9.4	3.8	5.7	3.4	7.9	6.0	3.2	4.9	2.7	2.9	3.3
DK	10.7	10.1	5.1	3.4	3.8	4.3	3.8	1.9	3.2	3.3	4.2	4.6
D	9.1	5.8	3.5	6.9	3.6	5.9	10.7	4.3	3.2	3.9	3.9	3.2
GR	10.1	21.6	15.5	11.2	9.6	13.8	10.3	9.4	12.3	9.8	8.7	7.5
E	14.6	18.0	7.7	8.1	4.4	8.2	9.3	6.8	4.6	3.9	4.4	4.6
F	9.9	12.9	4.2	3.6	2.9	4.3	4.3	2.2	2.1	3.0	3.2	3.2
IRL	11.3	16.6	6.0	5.2	3.2	3.8	7.0	4.9	3.2	2.7	3.2	3.6
I	11.5	18.2	8.8	5.9	4.4	8.5	5.8	3.6	3.4	4.7	4.9	4.6
L	7.4	9.2	5.1	5.4	4.1	4.8	6.2	5.3	4.5	3.7	3.9	4.2
NL	11.4	6.7	1.7	4.1	2.4	4.5	4.7	3.1	2.3	3.1	1.8	2.2
A	9.6	7.9	4.4	5.6	3.7	6.4	5.9	4.6	3.0	4.0	3.8	4.1
P	10.9	24.1	16.4	11.0	4.8	14.7	9.4	9.1	4.8	6.0	4.5	3.8
FIN	11.2	13.4	8.8	2.8	4.3	5.7	1.9	1.0	3.5	5.5	3.8	4.2
S	8.4	10.7	9.2	4.8	4.9	6.8	3.9	3.7	5.9	3.3	5.6	5.0
UK	8.3	13.9	8.2	6.3	3.4	8.6	5.5	4.9	2.8	3.2	3.8	3.8
EUR	9.9	12.4	6.1	6.0	3.7	6.9	6.9	4.1	3.3	3.7	3.9	3.7
USA	5.6	7.5	4.4	4.5	3.0	4.6	5.3	3.5	3.2	3.1	2.6	3.0
JAP	14.2	8.3	4.0	2.3	1.4	4.6	1.5	0.8	1.7	1.3	1.3	1.5

*Projections.

Source: European Commission services.

TABLE 4-5: Real Compensation of Employees Per Head (Percentage Change on Preceding Year, 1961–97)

	1961-73	1974-85	1986-90	1991-93	1994-97	1991	1992	1993	1994	1995	1996	1997*
B	5.1	1.8	1.5	3.1	1.1	5.3	4.0	0.1	1.8	1.1	0.5	1.1
DK	3.8	0.5	1.4	1.6	1.7	1.8	2.0	0.9	2.2	1.3	1.7	1.8
D	5.4	1.4	2.0	2.6	1.3	1.9	5.6	0.3	0.5	2.1	1.7	1.0
GR	6.4	3.5	-0.4	-4.0	0.8	-4.2	-4.1	-3.7	1.3	0.5	0.8	0.5
E	7.6	2.3	1.0	1.9	0.0	1.7	2.8	1.2	-0.5	-0.9	0.5	1.0
F	4.9	2.2	1.3	0.9	0.9	1.1	1.9	0.1	0.3	1.1	1.1	1.3
IRL	4.7	2.5	2.7	2.8	0.7	1.0	4.4	3.1	0.4	0.2	0.8	1.2
I	6.3	1.9	2.7	0.1	-0.2	1.5	0.4	-1.4	-1.3	-0.9	0.6	0.9
L	4.2	1.7	2.3	3.0	1.7	2.3	6.1	0.8	1.9	1.7	1.7	1.7
NL	6.0	0.9	0.8	1.2	0.4	1.2	1.5	0.8	0.0	1.5	0.0	0.2
A	5.3	1.9	2.4	1.9	1.2	2.8	1.9	1.1	0.0	1.5	1.5	1.7
P	6.7	1.6	4.2	0.7	0.6	1.8	-1.5	1.9	-0.7	1.7	0.8	0.5
FIN	5.2	2.4	4.1	-1.7	2.5	0.0	-2.2	-3.0	2.2	4.3	1.8	1.9
S	3.5	0.4	2.5	-1.1	2.0	-3.0	1.7	-2.0	2.7	0.5	2.9	1.9
UK	3.3	1.7	3.1	1.1	0.6	1.1	0.8	1.4	0.4	0.2	0.7	1.1
EUR	5.0	1.5	1.8	1.2	0.7	1.3	2.1	0.1	0.1	0.6	0.9	1.0
USA	2.5	0.4	0.3	1.4	0.8	0.8	2.4	1.1	1.0	0.8	0.6	0.7
JAP	7.6	1.8	3.0	0.3	1.1	2.1	-0.6	-0.4	1.4	1.7	1.0	0.5

*Projections.

Source: European Commission services.

37

TABLE 4-6: Total Employment (Percentage Change on Preceding Year, 1961–97)

	1961-73	1974-85	1986-90	1991-93	1994-97	1991	1992	1993	1994	1995	1996	1997*
B	0.6	-0.3	1.1	-0.6	0.1	0.1	-0.4	-1.4	-0.7	0.1	0.4	0.7
DK	1.1	0.5	0.3	-0.9	1.0	-1.5	-0.4	-0.7	-0.2	2.1	1.2	1.1
D	0.3	-0.2	1.5	-0.4	0.4	2.5	-1.8	-1.8	-0.7	0.0	0.7	1.5
GR	-0.5	1.0	0.7	0.0	1.3	-2.3	1.4	1.0	1.9	1.0	1.0	1.2
E	0.7	-1.4	3.3	-1.5	1.4	0.6	-1.2	-4.0	-0.9	2.5	1.9	2.0
F	0.7	0.1	0.8	-0.6	0.8	0.1	-0.7	-1.1	0.1	1.1	1.0	1.0
IRL	0.1	0.1	1.0	0.4	2.3	0.0	0.4	0.6	2.6	3.5	1.6	1.4
I	-0.2	0.9	0.6	-1.0	-0.1	0.8	-1.0	-2.6	-1.6	0.1	0.5	0.6
L	1.1	0.5	3.1	2.8	2.3	4.1	2.5	1.8	1.3	2.5	2.8	2.6
NL	0.9	-0.2	1.9	0.7	1.1	1.3	1.0	-0.2	0.1	1.2	1.4	1.8
A	-0.1	0.7	0.7	0.6	0.4	1.7	0.5	-0.4	0.3	0.2	0.3	0.8
P	0.3	-0.4	1.1	-0.3	0.2	2.8	-1.8	-1.9	-0.2	-0.6	0.5	1.1
FIN	0.5	0.3	0.2	-6.2	1.7	-5.2	-7.0	-6.5	-1.3	3.0	2.8	2.5
S	0.6	0.8	1.0	-3.9	0.7	-1.5	-4.4	-5.6	-1.0	1.7	1.0	1.0
UK	0.3	-0.2	1.8	-2.2	0.7	-3.1	-2.1	-1.6	0.7	0.8	0.7	0.6
EUR	0.3	0.0	1.3	-1.1	0.6	0.1	-1.4	-1.9	-0.4	0.7	0.9	1.1
USA	1.9	1.8	2.1	0.2	2.0	-1.0	-0.2	1.8	3.1	1.7	1.5	1.9
JAP	1.3	0.7	1.5	1.2	0.3	2.1	1.1	0.4	0.0	0.0	0.1	0.8

*Projections.
Source: European Commission services.

TABLE 4-7: Employment in Manufacturing Industries (Percentage Change on Preceding Year, 1961–97)

	1961-73	1974-85	1986-90	1991-93	1994-97	1991	1992	1993	1994	1995	1996	1997*
B	9.0	9.4	3.8	5.7	3.4	7.9	6.0	3.2	4.9	2.7	2.9	3.3
DK	10.7	10.1	5.1	3.4	3.8	4.3	3.8	1.9	3.2	3.3	4.2	4.6
D	9.1	5.8	3.5	6.9	3.6	5.9	10.7	4.3	3.2	3.9	3.9	3.2
GR	10.1	21.6	16.6	11.2	9.6	13.8	10.3	9.4	12.3	9.8	8.7	7.5
E	14.6	18.0	7.7	8.1	4.4	8.2	9.3	6.8	4.6	3.9	4.4	4.6
F	9.9	12.9	4.2	3.6	2.9	4.3	4.3	2.2	2.1	3.0	3.2	3.2
IRL	11.3	16.6	6.0	5.2	3.2	3.8	7.0	4.9	3.2	2.7	3.2	3.6
I	11.5	18.2	8.8	5.9	4.4	8.5	5.8	3.6	3.4	4.7	4.9	4.6
L	7.4	9.2	5.1	5.4	4.1	4.8	6.2	5.3	4.5	3.7	3.9	4.2
NL	11.4	6.7	1.7	4.1	2.4	4.5	4.7	3.1	2.3	3.1	1.8	2.2
A	9.6	7.9	4.4	5.6	3.7	6.4	5.9	4.6	3.0	4.0	3.8	4.1
P	10.9	24.1	16.4	11.0	4.8	14.7	9.4	9.1	4.8	6.0	4.5	3.8
FIN	11.2	13.4	8.8	2.8	4.3	5.7	1.9	1.0	3.5	5.5	3.8	4.2
S	8.4	10.7	9.2	4.8	4.9	6.8	3.9	3.7	5.9	3.3	5.6	5.0
UK	8.3	13.9	8.2	6.3	3.4	8.6	5.5	4.9	2.8	3.2	3.8	3.8
EUR	9.9	12.4	6.1	6.0	3.7	6.9	6.9	4.1	3.3	3.7	3.9	3.7
USA	5.6	7.5	4.4	4.5	3.0	4.6	5.3	3.5	3.2	3.1	2.6	3.0
JAP	14.2	8.3	4.0	2.3	1.4	4.6	1.5	0.8	1.7	1.3	1.3	1.5

*Projections.

Source: European Commission services.

39

TABLE 4-8: Exports of Goods (Percentage Volume Change on Preceding Year, 1974–97)

	1974-85	1986-90	1991-93	1994-97	1991	1992	1993	1994	1995	1996	1997*
B	2.7	6.2	2.6	6.1	1.7	4.2	1.8	7.8	5.4	5.5	5.7
DK	4.9	3.7	3.4	5.9	7.2	5.0	-1.7	8.2	4.5	5.2	5.7
D (Germany)	4.7	4.8	2.0	6.4	11.0	0.4	-4.8	9.2	4.4	5.3	6.6
GR	6.5	5.9	6.9	4.8	14.6	7.2	-0.5	3.0	5.3	5.5	5.5
E	8.5	5.2	9.2	10.5	10.0	6.7	11.0	20.7	9.0	6.3	6.4
F	4.3	5.1	2.5	6.5	3.9	4.7	-1.0	6.5	8.0	5.5	6.0
IRL	8.7	9.0	10.0	10.3	4.9	15.6	9.8	14.9	10.7	8.5	7.3
I	5.3	5.4	4.9	10.3	1.6	4.2	9.1	10.9	14.5	8.8	6.9
L	1.9	5.1	-0.3	5.1	3.1	0.2	-4.0	7.1	4.3	4.4	4.7
NL	3.3	5.3	2.7	6.5	4.8	2.6	0.6	6.8	7.0	6.4	5.8
A	6.3	7.8	3.2	7.9	6.5	2.2	1.0	8.0	8.1	7.6	7.9
P	NA	11.9	0.4	12.1	0.5	6.1	-5.1	14.9	12.3	12.8	8.5
FIN	3.7	1.6	6.4	8.8	-5.9	9.3	17.0	13.1	12.1	5.3	5.1
S	3.1	2.5	2.8	11.4	-2.5	1.3	9.9	15.8	13.5	9.1	7.3
UK	3.9	5.4	2.3	7.5	1.2	2.5	3.2	9.9	6.2	7.0	6.7
EUR	4.7	5.4	3.6	7.7	5.2	3.5	2.1	9.9	7.9	6.6	6.5
USA	2.5	10.4	6.5	10.7	7.5	6.6	5.5	11.4	13.5	9.0	9.0
JAP	9.0	2.6	0.7	5.0	2.3	0.7	-1.0	1.5	6.0	6.0	6.5

*Projections.

Source: European Commission services.

40

TABLE 4-9: European External Balance (Percent of GDP)

	1993	1994	Forecast 1995	1996	Scenario 1997
Trade balance	1.0	1.3	1.7	1.8	2.0
Services balance	0.3	0.3	0.3	0.2	0.2
Factor income and transfers	-1.3	-1.2	-1.5	-1.5	-1.5
Current account balance	0.0	0.3	0.5	0.6	0.7

Source: European Commission services.

TABLE 4-10: World Trade Balances (Fob-fob, in Billions U.S. Dollars)

	1992	1993	1994	1995	1996	1997*
EUR	-9.5	70.9	99.1	140.7	161.1	184.7
USA	-96.1	-132.6	-166.4	-189.0	-202.4	-210.0
Japan	132.4	141.6	145.9	141.5	141.3	136.4
Canada	6.0	7.6	12.8	15.4	17.3	17.8
Rest OECD	4.0	-2.4	4.4	-1.8	-1.3	-1.2
CCEE (Central/Eastern Europe)	-8.8	-3.3	-1.1	-5.8	-6.0	-5.5
OPEC	39.9	45.0	50.4	54.4	46.3	60.1
Other developing countries	21.4	3.6	8.6	-53.4	-55.3	-62.4
—DAEs†	-2.5	-3.0	-10.7	-20.6	-22.2	-26.2
—Other Asia	-14.1	-28.3	-14.6	-3.1	0.1	-0.7
—Latin America	8.0	-1.0	-5.6	-16.7	-19.4	-20.6
—Africa	-9.9	-9.0	-10.9	-13.0	-13.8	-14.9

* Projections.
† DAEs—Dynamic Asian Economies (Hong Kong, Korea, Malaysia, Singapore, Taiwan, Thailand).

Source: European Commission services.

5 THE EUROPEAN MONETARY SYSTEM AND THE COMMON CURRENCY: CONTRIBUTION TO REGIONAL INTEGRATION?

The economic and social integration of the EU depends to a major degree on the establishment of a successful monetary system and eventually a common currency (the Euro). This task is awesome, given the continuing strong nationalistic tendencies among EU member states, and requires skillful strategies that have shown some success.

Historically, the Hague Conference of December 1969 introduced a commitment by the six EC governments at that time to adopt a schedule for economic and monetary union. In June of 1970, the Community adopted the Werner Plan, named after its author, the prime minister of Luxembourg. Its aim was to introduce a three-stage, ten-year schedule for an economic and monetary union, involving in the economic field obligatory consultations on short- and medium-term planning, coordination of budgeting, harmonization of fiscal policies, cooperation of central banks in narrowing currency fluctuations, movement to a stabilization fund for currency aid, and establishment of supranational institutions by 1989.[1]

These objectives were not achieved fully. In 1978 French President Valery Giscard d'Estaing and German Chancellor Helmut Schmidt, who had very similar ideas about the future of the European political and economic system, sought a "zone of monetary stability" as a realistic goal, and by the mid-1980s the European Monetary System (EMS) had become a quasi-fixed exchange rate regime facilitating trade and commerce among the member states,[2] but the achievement of a true common currency was not yet in sight.

It is important to understand the principle of the EMS: Not all member states participated on the same level. At the center of the EMS was an accounting currency, the European Currency Unit (ECU), which was a basket for all the EMS currencies. Most of the national currencies of the EU members were participating in the Exchange Rate Mechanism (ERM). Exceptions in 1996 were Great Britain, Greece, Portugal, and Italy, but the latter has negotiated readmission.[3]

Three institutions play important roles in the operation of EMS, now better known as the European Monetary Union (EMU): the Monetary Committee, the Committee of Central Bank Governors, and the Banking Advisory Committee. The Monetary Committee deals with the preparation of monetary decisions within the EU; parity changes are the most visible activities. Final action is mostly taken within the Council of Economics and Finance Ministers. The Committee of Central Bank Governors is a consultative body. Although the Werner Report recommended increasing the power of the Committee, it was actually nothing more than a forum for the exchange of views. The Banking Advisory Committee is of little direct importance in the conduct of EU monetary policy; it pursues an independent commitment to European identity and the completion of the single market.

Later, in the beginning of the 1990s, two other institutions were set up: the European Monetary Institute (EMI),[4] located in Frankfurt, Germany, which was to be the forerunner of the European Central Bank, and the European System of Central Banks, in which the European Central Bank would coexist with the current national central banks in a semi-federal structure. During this period the new Central Bank would assume important monetary responsibilities, and this coordinated activity would strengthen economic policy implementation, which would now include the European Monetary Union (EMU).[5]

CONVERGENCE REQUIREMENTS AND RESULTS

The Treaty on European Union requires that convergence on certain economic data must be undertaken (Article 109j and the associated protocol) in order to ensure, eventually, a common currency for a majority of EU member states. The criteria involved in the convergence exercise are a strong budgetary performance, a high degree of price stability, specified long-term interest rates, and participation in the ERM. Some of these concerns were discussed in chapter 4, in which we also analyzed the problem of unemployment, a serious matter for a common currency because of possible future uncertainties. Participation in the ERM also had suffered, especially in September 1992 during the crisis of major currencies, which led to the withdrawal of the United Kingdom and Italy from ERM, although Italy has now rejoined this organization.

Table 5-1 provides data on convergence for 1995, and these data are not very encouraging—especially as far as excessive budgetary deficits are concerned. But as we have already noted, some member states are making intense efforts to see the common currency start in 1999 and Germany, led by its chancellor Helmut Kohl, is in the forefront of this endeavor. But many Germans are fearful to abandon the Mark, which is considered the emblem of prosperity and stability. Chancellor Kohl hopes that his population will change its mind through a huge campaign emphasizing that the Euro will be as strong as the Mark.[6] France and the Benelux countries support this objective and are preparing themselves to attain the convergence data necessary to participate in the Euro currency in 1999 (see Table 5-1).

According to an interim, informal assessment of convergence achievements in the terms of the Treaty criteria up to the end of 1995, the situation was largely satisfactory as far as inflation and interest rates were concerned, but much less so regarding budgetary performance, with only Germany, Ireland, and Luxembourg not having an excessive deficit. A first formal examination of the fulfillment of the convergence criteria was made in the reports prepared by the Commission and the EMI before the end of 1996.[7]

The same group of member states that had inflation at or below the reference value in 1994 (B, DK, D, F, IRL, I, NL, UK) continued to do so in 1995; in addition, this group was enlarged by the three new member states (A, FIN, S), which also respected the criterion. Inflation convergence has been notable among the member states which have long participated in the ERM and were in the narrow band prior to August 1993 when membership expanded (B, DK, D, F, IRL, NL). Four member states (GR, E, I, P) still have inflation rates above the reference value, but in recent years they have narrowed the gap between their inflation performance and that of the others. In 1995 the inflation rate came down substantially in Greece (but it still remains very high) and Portugal, and more gradually in Spain, but in Italy in 1997 there was an increase in the inflation rate. In these countries (and several others) exchange rate depreciation added to cost pressures, but the effects on domestic prices were more moderate than in the experience of earlier decades.

Less progress has been made in budgetary convergence. Only three member states (D, IRL, and L) do not currently have an excessive deficit according to the terms of the Treaty (Article 104c). The recovery in economic activity and discretionary budgetary adjustment measures made roughly equal contributions to the reduction in the deficit in the EU as a whole in 1995, but the pace of adjustment has not been fast enough, and most member states in excessive deficit are faced with the need to implement significant additional adjustment measures in order to satisfy the budgetary convergence criteria. While deficits have generally been reduced, only four member states (DK, D, IRL, and L) were estimated to have deficits below 3 percent of GDP in 1995.

Trends in government debt ratios continue to be unsatisfactory in most member states, but the sharp deterioration recorded in the early 1990s has eased; several member states have already stabilized their gross debt ratios, and others are close to doing so. Indeed, of the eleven member states with gross debt ratios higher than the 60 percent of GDP reference value, four are likely to achieve a reduction in the ratio in 1997.

Convergence in long-term interest rates remained largely unchanged in 1995. Interest rates rose at the beginning of the year, reflecting turbulence in foreign exchange markets and tensions in the ERM. Reductions have taken place since, which have been particularly pronounced in those member states already with low interest rates. Long-term interest rates in the Community have generally remained higher than the average levels reached in 1994 when eight of the twelve member states respected the criterion. Nevertheless, in 1995, ten of the fifteen member states had long-term interest rates below the reference value for this criterion. The larger group this year includes two of the new member states (A and FIN). Improving long-term interest rate convergence will require further progress in resolving budgetary uncertainties and in securing price stability in a lasting manner.

Notable progress in financial integration has been achieved by the member states and, since June 1994, a regime of free movement of capital prevails in the Union. This has contributed substantially to easing the financing of external deficits and to easing the external constraints.

The Treaty on European Union sets out four explicit criteria according to which nominal convergence can be measured (Article 109j[8] and the associated protocol). At the same time, however, the Treaty requires that the assessment of convergence take into account evidence from other pertinent indicators, which would permit emergence of a broader picture of the progress toward stability and integration between the member states. Of these indices, a set refers to what may be regarded as indicators of the sustainability of nominal convergence. In this regard, the present report also reviews developments in unit labor costs and in import prices, as well as developments in the current account.

We have mentioned in the preceding chapters that a common currency in the CU would reduce the cost of interstate transactions. An example is the elimination of transfer commissions for the change of one national currency into another when payment is made for goods, or simply to acquire a particular amount of currency in another EU state for any purpose. This is one reason why multinational enterprises and large business organizations in many EU states are anxious for the establishment of a common currency and lobby for such an event—even in the United Kingdom, despite the activities of powerful Eurosceptics.

While the conversion criteria of the Maastricht Treaty provide valuable guidelines for the EMU, a clear and unequivocal commitment not only by the EU governments, but also by the major political parties, employers, and unions—as well as the general public—is an important prerequisite for establishing EMU, because non-EMU countries can engage in competitive devaluations for increased exports.[9]

The concern here is about the regional integration process in Europe, and the question may be raised whether EMU can be installed without a federalized EU, or what kind of minimal EU structure would suffice to obtain the advantages of EMU—such as agreements on public deficits and a high degree of price stability. At the same time, the relations between EMU members and nonmembers will require continuing analysis, as they may nurture different treatment between activities of EMU banks and non-EMU banks in participating EU countries—for example, the Bank of England. Perhaps we should keep in mind a slow movement from *Gesellschaft* as it exists at present, toward *Gemeinschaft*, as discussed in a previous chapter. The successful introduction of EMU and a common currency may provide the needed impetus for the movement to *Gemeinschaft* in the EU, highlighting the economic and social advantages of a more integrated community and eventually weakening the nationalistic tendencies among EU populations. It is interesting to note that some banks in Denmark, which is basically opposed to EMU, fear that they would be at a competitive disadvantage if their country would stay out of the European Monetary Union and the Euro payments and settlements system known as TARGET.[10] The United Kingdom is also concerned about TARGET, and its government is giving second thoughts to eventually joining the common currency in the EU. Both the Confederation of British Industry and the British Chamber of Commerce are preparing to establish a joint working group to assess the impact on business if the United Kingdom joined or stayed outside EMU.[11] But despite the fact that London may be the most important financial center in Europe, the Bank of England has refused to establish a steering committee to prepare the United Kingdom for monetary union because of political uncertainty about belonging to EMU. On the other hand, the Bank of France considers that the French financial groups must prepare themselves now for using the Euro as soon as possible after EMU starts in 1999.[12] Belgium and Finland are also eager to become members of the common currency as soon as possible and have begun a process of reducing their debt portfolios.[13] But there are also negative cost considerations influencing the initiation of EMU. EU retailers could face substantial costs, perhaps $21.4 billion, in adapting their operations to the introduction of the Euro. Moreover, it may well be difficult to sell citizens in the EU on the introduction of the common currency if, as a result of this step, prices would increase.[14] What we see, then, is considerable political pressure to maintain the schedule for the introduction of the common currency, but also strong arguments for postponing this event.[15]

The *Financial Times* has developed a listing of countries that seek admission to the common currency system if and when it is established, and shows prospects of success. Only France, Germany, and Belgium seem to be assured participation, but we need to keep in mind that some other countries—such as Italy—will do as much as possible financial engineering to qualify for EMU participation.

There is no doubt that most detailed news on the EU can be gleaned from the *Financial Times*. But one must also recognize that the *Financial Times* pursues certain aims in its pages that do not fully support EMU but may at times work for delays beyond the starting date of 1999. In the meantime it has been publishing periodically data developed by J.P. Morgan as to the probabilities of prominent EU member states becoming EMU members. An example is shown in Table 5-2.

A very important factor in the complex common currency initiation is the completion of the IGC, which was slated to occur in Italy in the spring of 1996 with an opening in Turin. But it quickly became obvious that, despite additional meetings in other Italian cities, the conclusion of the IGC had to await at least the European Council meeting in Ireland during the second half of 1996, most likely the Council session in the Netherlands in the first half of 1997, and maybe the session in Luxembourg during the second half of that year. The outcome of the British elections on May 1, 1997, is likely to affect seriously the outcome of the IGC. The Dutch presidency of the European Council seeks to improve the institutional effectiveness in the EU, to set up a new exchange rate system between the Euro and currencies of non-Euro countries, and to emphasize social policy and greater labor market efficiency.[16]

A stability and growth pact was accepted in 1996 to prevent EMU participants from running lax budgetary policies. While it provided for sanctions against offenders, these may never be applied because of the powerful disincentive against running excessive deficits that have been built into the pact through the implementation of reinforced stability programs. The main points of agreement between ministers were:

- EMU members' fiscal policies should aim at broad balance. Deficits should not exceed 3 percent of GDP, except in "exceptional and temporary circumstances."
- Each EMU member will submit to the Council of Ministers and the Commission a stability program that will include medium-term objectives that may be updated regularly. This will set fiscal objectives and indicate the evolution of public debt as a proportion of GDP. It will set out the main assumptions about expected economic developments, describe the budgetary measures being taken to achieve the budgetary objectives, and commit each government to taking additional measures to prevent slippage from these targets.
- Stability programs must be endorsed by the Council which, if it so decides, may indicate ways in which the program should be strengthened. If a member state registers a deficit above 3 percent and fails to act on Council recommendations to correct the slippage within the subsequent calendar year, it will face sanctions in the form of an interest-free deposit that must be lodged with the EU. This would be converted into a fine if no action is eventually taken within two years.

The new version of the ERM will be designed to avoid instability between the Euro and the currencies of member states not participating in EMU as of 1 January 1999—frequently known as the "pre-ins." A "hub and spokes" arrangement with the Euro at its center, the new system will seek to be flexible while encouraging the EU countries expected in the second wave of EMU members to maintain convergence policies that will enable them to qualify for EMU as soon as possible.[17]

The Commissioner for Economic, Financial, and Monetary Affairs, Yves-Thibault de Silguy, discussed the significance of the stability pact during the IGC in Dublin and stated that "It gives full expression to the Treaty procedures designed to maintain the strength and credibility of the Euro. Although a lot of attention has been given to the system deterrence effect of sanctions against a Member State whose fiscal policies are not sufficiently disciplined, the procedures should prevent such a situation arising. The pact should give investors confidence that the Euro is underpinned by policies and procedures which guarantee durable sound management of public finances."[18]

Relevant information on these issues may be provided by public opinion surveys, which will be explored in the next chapter.

NOTES

[1]Charles Pentland, *International Theory and European Integration* (New York: The Free Press, 1973), pp. 140–41.

[2]David R. Carmeron, "The 1992 Initiative: Causes and Consequences," in *Euro-Politics*, ed. Alberta M. Skragia (Washington, DC: The Brookings Institution, 1991), pp. 45–47.

[3]See John T. Wooley, "Policy Credibility and European Monetary Institutions," in *Euro-Politics,* ed. Alberta M. Skragia (Washington, DC: The Brookings Institution, 1991), pp. 161–70.

[4]For the details of the Monetary Committee see the "Protocol on the European Monetary Institute" (EMI), *Maastricht Treaty*, pp. 172–82.

[5]For details see Neill Nugent, *The Government and Politics of the European Community*, 2nd ed. (Durham, NC: Duke University Press, 1991), pp. 255–57.

[6]*New York Times*, 12 July, 1996, p. A4, and the *Financial Times*, 6–7 July, 1996, p. 1.

[7]See European Commission, *European Economy*, Supplement A, January 1996.

[8]In November 1993, and in accordance with Article 109e(2)b of the Treaty, the Commission adopted the "Report on progress with regard to economic and monetary convergence and with the implementation of Community law concerning the internal market," *European Economy*, no. 55, 1993. In 1994 the review of convergence was presented in Convergence Report 1994: "Achieving better convergence during a period of economic recovery," *European Economy* no. 59, 1995.

[9]See *Financial Times*, 9 July, 1996, p. 2, and 5 July, 1996, p. 1, dealing with competitive advantages of non-EMU countries vis-á-vis EMU countries.

[10]See *New York Times*, 15 April, 1996, pp. 13, 15.

[11]*Financial Times*, 30 July, 1996, p. 6.

[12]*Financial Times*, 1 August, 1996, p. 10. See also the next chapter, on public opinions.

[13]*Financial Times*, 25 July, 1996, p. 1, and 26 July, 1996, p. 17, 24.

[14]*Financial Times*, 25 October, 1996, p. 16.

[15]*New York Times*, 30 August, 1996, p. C3.

[16]*European Report*, no. 2187, 4 January, 1997, p. 1.

[17]*Infeuro*, no. 1 (November 1996), pp. 1–2.

[18]*Infeuro*, no. 1 (November 1996), p. 3.

TABLE 5-1: Performance of the Member States in Relation to Convergence in 1995

| | Inflation | | General government budgetary position | | | | | Long-term interest rates | Exchange rates |
| | Private consumption deflator | Consumer price index | Existence of an excessive deficit | Deficit/GDP | Debt/GDP | Change | | | ERM participation |
	1995	Oct.1994-Sept.1995	Council decisions 9.26.94 & 7.10.95	1995	1995	95/94	95/93	Nov.1995	Nov.1995
Reference value:	2.9	3.0		3.0	60			10.4	
B	1.5	1.6	yes	4.5	134.4	-0.6	-3.1	7.0	yes
DK	2.0	2.2	yes	2.0	73.6	-2.0	-6.7	8.6	yes
D	1.8	2.2	no	2.9	58.8	8.6	10.6	7.1	yes
GR	9.2	9.9	yes	9.3	114.4	1.4	-0.1	18.4	no
E	4.9	4.7	yes	5.9	64.8	1.8	4.4	11.5	yes
F	1.9	1.7	yes	5.0	51.5	3.1	6.2	7.8	yes
IRL	2.5	2.6[1]	no	2.7	85.9	-5.2	-11.5	8.5	yes
I	5.6	4.7	yes	7.4	124.9	-0.5	5.5	12.3	no
L	1.9	2.1	no	-0.4	6.4	0.5	0.1	6.2	yes
NL	1.6	2.2	yes	3.1	78.4	0.4	-2.9	7.2	yes
A	2.4	2.5	yes	5.5	68.0	2.8	5.0	7.3	yes
P	4.2	4.2	yes	5.4	70.5	1.1	3.3	11.7	yes
FIN	1.2	1.3	yes	5.4	63.2	3.4	5.9	9.4	no
S	2.8	2.6	yes	7.0	81.4	1.7	5.2	10.7	no
UK	2.9	3.3	yes	5.1	52.5	2.4	3.9	8.4	no
EUR	3.1	3.3		4.7	71.0	2.9	4.8	8.1	

1. Measured on the basis of quarterly data.

TABLE 5-2: EMU—Who's Going to Make It? (J.P. Morgan Calculator February 17, 1997)

	Feb. 16, 1997	Feb. 9, 1997	Jan. 19, 1997
Germany	100%	100%	100%
France	100%	100%	100%
Belgium	100%	100%	100%
Spain	65%	74%	83%
Sweden	64%	66%	76%
Italy	62%	63%	74%
Denmark	38%	39%	56%
United Kingdom	31%	45%	42%

The EMU calculator provides a weekly snapshot of the probabilities which the financial markets place on selected countries being willing and able to join Germany in forming a single European currency in 1999. Currency strategists at the J.P. Morgan Investment Bank calculate the probabilities from the interest rate swaps market, in which investors swap floating rate interest payments on an investment for fixed-rate ones. Countries are selected if they have a liquid swaps market that allows comparable probabilities to be calculated. The Netherlands is seen as being 100 percent certain of joining EMU. Finland, Ireland, and Portugal will be added to the EMU calculator in late 1997.

EMU expectations have decreased recently outside Europe's hard core countries, as the markets reassess the likelihood of a wide EMU arriving in 1999.

Source: Financial Times, 17 February, 1997.

6 PUBLIC OPINIONS: DIRECTION AND IMPACT REGARDING EU INTEGRATION

In chapter 3, discussing the aspects of democracy for the EU, I suggested that the possible vagaries of public opinion could have a positive effect in assuring a democratic system underlying the management and decision making of the Union. If a movement from *Gesellschaft* to *Gemeinschaft* in the operation of the EU could be detected in the public opinions over a period of time, the approach to eliminating the democratic deficit in the operation of the EU may be more successful. We will use selected data from the *Eurobarometer* Vol. 45 (Spring 1996) and Vol. 46, (Autumn 1996) issues, to offer an appropriate analysis and seek to obtain a comprehensive picture of public opinion through *Eurobarometer Trends* information. The data included in the trend volumes have been published every year since 1990, and our current source appeared in November 1994 covering the years 1974 through 1994.

A main issue in evaluating public opinion is the kind of support that may be given by interviewees regarding a particular policy. Support, if indicated by the interview subjects, may flow from affective or utilitarian sources. "Affective" support stems from an emotional attachment to the principles of integration, while "utilitarian" support results from a cost-benefit analysis of the impact of integration on the respondent's own situation.[1] Utilitarian support is most likely more effective as it includes the interests of large multinational and national business enterprises as well as associations of EU companies and unions. Affective support may benefit from trends toward regional organization, as strengthening these organizations may depend on increasing cooperation with EU top management structures.

The questions asked by the *Eurobarometer* are far-ranging, and not all responses can be related to the support of individual interviewees. Nevertheless, the tables and figures selected provide interesting insights into the public opinion that exists regarding specific political issues affecting the future of the EU, and what structural changes in the Maastricht Treaty may be acceptable to the EU member governments. The *Eurobarometer* 46 (Autumn 1996) provides a list of highlights (p. III), which provides a general indication of the direction public opinion was taking in the EU at that time.

SPECIFIC *EUROBAROMETER* QUESTIONS AND RESPONSES

Of key interest are the issues of unification of Western Europe (support) and benefits of EU membership. Tables 6-1, 6-2, 6-3, and 6-4 provide the answers from the relevant interviews. The unification of Western Europe is very much supported by 21 percent of respondents in all 15 EU member states and 48 percent "to some extent." Against unification are 24 percent (8 percent very much) and 6 percent don't know. Luxembourg, Ireland, Italy, and France show the strongest overall support, and the United Kingdom shows the weakest (57 percent). With respect to the demographical breakdown of the respondents, it is interesting to note that those with extended and higher education are in the forefront of unification supporters. The same is found with opinion leaders and the other top-level occupations such as managers and other white collar employees.

Another significant question asked is whether membership in the EU is a good or bad thing. Among the respondents in the 15 member states, 53 percent considered it a good thing, 14 percent thought it was a bad thing, and 28 percent felt it was neither good nor bad (Table 6-3). Again, the most positive countries were the Netherlands, Ireland, and Luxembourg. The most negative responses came from Sweden, Austria, and the United Kingdom— 52 percent, 43 percent, and 46 percent respectively. The "neither good nor bad" responses were highest in Austria (43 percent), Portugal (32 percent), and Germany (35 percent). In terms of sociological indication, the men, best educated, opinion leaders, and managers expressed the most positive positions regarding membership in the European Union (Table 6-2).

Similar views were also expressed about benefits from EU membership (Tables 6-2 and 6-3). Forty-three percent of the respondents in the 15 EU member states answered positively, but a large percentage of more than one-third did not see any benefits, and 21 percent of the interviewees did not have any opinion, with one-quarter being aged 55 years of age and above. The least educated respondents made up the highest category of those not knowing about the EU membership impact, and in terms of occupation it was house workers who showed the least knowledge.

An important issue concerning the future is the economic situation in respondents' countries, hence a question asked dealt with their expectations about this issue. The responses in the EU as a whole were fairly optimistic (46 percent); 35 percent were fearful; 10 percent very fearful. For details see Table 6-4. Similar expressions were also recorded for employment, which was considered a key priority area for the EU. Eighty-five percent believed joint EU programs should be developed to fight against unemployment; 16 percent believed unemployment would be the same, and only 18 percent looked for improvement in job opportunities through the EU (Table 6-5 and Figure 6-1).

Finally, some questions in the interviews dealt with the desirability of a common currency and the need for a European government. The details can be found in Tables 6-6 and 6-7, and the responses are presented for the EU of 15 members and for individual countries.

A common EU currency is supported by 53 percent of the respondents (20 percent "very much," 33 percent "somewhat"), with Italy, Luxembourg, and Spain in the forefront. The opposition is strongest in Denmark and the United Kingdom, but it is also found in Germany, Austria, and Finland, although the German and Finnish governments are strong supporters (Table 6-6).

An elected European government is considered necessary by 54 percent of the respondents, but opposed most strongly in Denmark and Sweden (82 and 70 percent). Surprisingly, in Britain 39 percent considered it only "unnecessary."

Moving to other issue areas, support for having common foreign and defense policies was substantial (66 and 60 percent, respectively), but there was also opposition (20 and 26 percent), perhaps because a common foreign policy may touch on the exercise of national sovereignty by some member states. Sweden may be a case in point, with 44 percent opposition to a common foreign policy. We will discuss the problem in general in the next chapter.

TRENDS

Many items used for the *Eurobarometer*'s semi-annual test of public opinion are the basis for trend analyses. We will use two questions for this purpose: "attitudes toward support for European integration" from 1981 to 1995 and "attitudes toward a future European government responsible to the European Parliament" from 1987 to 1993. The answers to the first question were divided into for or against unification, and Figure 6-2 shows a steady but modest decline of support from 1990 to 1995 and a continuing, but again modest, increase of opponents to integration over the same years. The results in 1996 are 53 percent pro-integration and 15 percent against it.[2]

The second issue, regarding responsibility of governmental institutions in the EU to the European Parliament, relates to the importance of the principle of democracy for EU law-making and executive functions in the Union. The responses to these questions were favorable, mostly close to 50 percent of the interviewees, while the opponents scored about 25 percent and so did those who did not reply at all.[3] Denmark was most strongly opposed, 67 percent in 1992, and the United Kingdom was 57 percent against it in the same year.

In 1995 two questions were asked regarding the power of the EP in the legislative and executive functions. The first dealt with the responsibility of the European government to the EP and the European Council of Heads of State and Government. The response in the EU of 15 countries was 61 percent for and 16 percent opposed. Twenty-three percent "did not know." The second question posed a European government responsible only to the EP. Fifty-nine percent agreed, 18 percent were opposed, and 24 percent had no response.[4]

The *Eurobarometer* 46, as some previous compilations of EU public opinions, contains a list of highlights, some of which are very useful for gaining an overview of significant developments during the last few years. A number of these highlights are reproduced and provide interesting insights into recent EU developments as far as the views of the population are concerned. It is noteworthy that only 13 percent of the respondents consider enlargement to be an option for the immediate future, although some member governments such as Great Britain push this issue in order to prevent movement of the EU toward a federal structure.

HIGHLIGHTS

- Economic and social expectations for 1997 have been mainly pessimistic. Economic conditions in member states are not expected to improve. More positive exceptions are observed in Ireland, Finland, the Netherlands and the United Kingdom, where approximately one in three persons anticipated that 1997 would be a better year than 1996.
- Pessimism is highest in Germany, France, Belgium, and Greece, with only one in ten persons expecting improvements.

- Nearly one in two EU citizens expects the employment situation generally to deteriorate. Again pessimism runs particularly high in Germany, with 74 percent in East Germany and 65 percent in West Germany expecting the job market to get worse.
- Standard indicators show a drop in support for the European Union over the past twelve months. Support for membership has declined 5 percent; support remains highest, but shows no increase, in Ireland, Luxembourg, and the Netherlands, and is at its lowest in Sweden, Austria, the United Kingdom, Finland, and Germany.
- Support for issues relating to the democratic processes remains strong, and two-thirds of Europeans support the development of common defense and foreign policies.
- Support for a common European currency has increased by 4 percent in the past twelve months to 51 percent, but the vast majority (77 percent) of the general public feels ill informed, 2 percent feel very well informed, and 19 percent feel well informed. Those feeling informed tend to be men, the well educated, and from the higher socio-economic groups.
- Just over half (51 percent) of EU citizens describe themselves as European to some extent, but there has been a rise (+6 percent) in those considering themselves as "nationality only." The political left is more likely to regard itself as European than those considering themselves as belonging to the right—50 percent compared to 38 percent.
- Seven in ten EU citizens feel ill informed about the Union, and the majority, 67 percent, would like to learn more. Levels of knowledge concerning citizens' rights were varied: Certain areas such as the right to study and work in another member state were understood, but a number of other rights were less well known. The expected sources of information about the EU are television and the press, but in national contexts there are considerable differences; e.g., the Internet is cited by 42 percent in Sweden, but only 11 percent in Spain.

NOTES

[1]Vincent Mahler, Bruce Taylor, and Jennifer Wozinak, "Exploring the Relationship Between Economic Growth and Public Attitudes Toward European Integration," ECSA Conference, May 11–14, 1995. Sometimes the term "constitutional" support is used for "affective."

[2]For Details for individual member countries, see *European Commission, Eurobarometer, Variable Trends 1974–1993* (May 1994), pp. 50–67 and pp. 148–54.

[3]Ibid.

[4]See Table 6-8 for replies in the member states.

TABLE 6-1: Unification (Percent by Country)

Question: In general, are you for or against efforts being made to unify Western Europe? Are you . . . ?

Countries	For, very much	For, to some extent	Against, to some extent	Against, very much	Don't know	Total
EU15	21	48	16	8	8	100
B	15	53	19	6	6	100
DK	20	44	19	14	3	100
West D	20	43	20	9	7	100
D	18	43	21	10	7	100
East D	12	43	27	12	6	100
GR	29	49	10	6	6	100
E	21	54	10	4	11	100
F	18	52	15	7	8	100
IRL	32	49	6	2	11	100
I	31	54	6	2	7	100
L	32	50	10	3	5	100
NL	21	56	14	5	4	100
A	20	36	21	14	10	100
P	26	51	10	3	10	100
FIN	10	50	21	14	6	100
S	19	41	20	15	5	100
UK	14	41	21	14	10	100
EU12	21	49	15	7	8	100

Source: European Commission services.

TABLE 6-2: Membership (Percent by Country)

Question: Generally speaking, do you think that *(our country's)* membership in the European Union is . . . ?

Countries	A good thing	A bad thing	Neither good nor bad	Don't know	Total
EU15	53	14	28	6	100
B	54	15	29	3	100
DK	53	21	23	3	100
West D	47	13	33	7	100
D	46	13	35	7	100
East D	41	11	42	7	100
GR	58	8	30	3	100
E	54	13	29	5	100
F	53	13	29	5	100
IRL	77	4	14	5	100
I	69	6	17	8	100
L	73	7	18	2	100
NL	78	6	14	3	100
A	34	24	34	8	100
P	54	9	32	5	100
FIN	45	22	29	4	100
S	32	36	28	4	100
UK	41	21	30	8	100
EU12	54	13	28	6	100

Source: European Commission services.

TABLE 6-3: Benefit from Membership (Percent by Country)

Question: Taking everything into consideration, would you say that *(our country)* has, on balance, benefited or not from being a member of the European Union?

Countries	Benefited	Not benefited	Don't know	Total
EU15	43	36	21	100
B	41	36	23	100
DK	60	26	14	100
West D	39	41	20	100
D	38	41	21	100
East D	34	42	24	100
GR	65	24	11	100
E	39	39	23	100
F	41	36	23	100
IRL	85	5	9	100
I	49	25	26	100
L	63	18	18	100
NL	64	20	16	100
A	37	43	20	100
P	70	18	12	100
FIN	36	48	16	100
S	19	52	29	100
UK	33	46	21	100
EU12	43	35	21	100

Source: European Commission services.

TABLE 6-4: Single European Market: Hope or Fear? (Percent by Country)

Question: Personally, would you say that the Single European Market, which came about at the beginning of 1993, makes you feel . . . ?

Countries	Very hopeful	Rather hopeful	Rather fearful	Very fearful	Don't know	Total
EU15	8	46	25	10	12	100
B	9	47	22	11	11	100
DK	8	52	25	6	9	100
West D	11	40	29	9	12	100
D	10	39	30	10	12	100
East D	9	38	32	10	11	100
GR	14	57	13	7	9	100
E	7	49	21	5	18	100
F	9	42	24	18	7	100
IRL	19	55	7	2	18	100
I	7	52	23	9	9	100
L	18	51	15	3	13	100
NL	5	61	14	2	18	100
A	14	41	22	9	15	100
P	13	47	25	7	9	100
FIN	4	57	23	5	12	100
S	4	39	37	11	10	100
UK	5	42	27	10	16	100
EU12	8	46	24	10	12	100

Source: European Commission services.

TABLE 6-5: Employment As a Key Priority Area (Percent by Country)

Question: Some people expect the European Union to become (even) more active than now in certain areas. For each of the following, please tell me if you consider it a key priority or not. (Explanations for the four columns are shown at the end of the table.)

Countries	+: Key priority -: No key priority	m)	o)	z)	gg)
EU15	+	85	76	68	66
	-	11	17	25	24
B	+	81	80	61	62
	-	12	14	31	28
DK	+	64	61	70	53
	-	33	35	28	39
West D	+	83	69	56	58
	-	12	23	36	30
D	+	85	69	59	59
	-	10	23	33	30
East D	+	92	70	70	59
	-	4	20	23	29
GR	+	91	85	77	73
	-	7	12	18	20
E	+	90	81	77	76
	-	5	11	16	14
F	+	88	86	78	75
	-	9	10	19	18
IRL	+	88	81	75	74
	-	6	9	18	15
I	+	89	83	68	71
	-	6	10	24	18

TABLE 6-5 (continued)

Countries	+: Key priority -: No key priority	m)	o)	z)	gg)
L	+	82	79	75	77
	-	12	15	18	12
NL	+	79	68	73	68
	-	19	29	26	29
A	+	81	64	60	56
	-	12	25	28	29
P	+	87	76	70	70
	-	7	15	23	18
FIN	+	86	81	63	67
	-	11	14	32	26
S	+	81	74	68	68
	-	16	20	27	24
UK	+	76	70	64	56
	-	17	22	28	33
EU12	+	85	77	68	66
	-	10	17	25	24
UE15	+	85	76	68	66
	-	11	17	25	24

m) Developing joint programs to fight against unemployment.
o) Providing more opportunities to find a job anywhere in the European Union.
z) Improving equality of opportunity between men and women.
gg) Improving equality of opportunities for minorities.

Source: European Commission services.

TABLE 6-6: European Currency: For or Against? (Percent by Country)

Question: Are you for or against the European Union having one European currency in all member states, including *(our country)*? That is, replacing the *(name of national currency)* with the European currency? Are you . . . ?

Countries	Very much for	Somewhat for	Somewhat against	Very much against	Neither for, nor against (spontaneous)	Don't know	Total
EU15	20	33	15	18	9	6	100
B	17	36	12	10	19	5	100
DK	17	19	21	37	4	2	100
West D	13	28	22	26	5	6	100
D	13	27	23	26	5	6	100
East D	12	26	26	26	5	6	100
GR	33	31	10	11	8	8	100
E	22	40	9	6	12	11	100
F	22	37	12	10	14	4	100
IRL	33	33	10	6	8	11	100
I	33	45	6	3	8	5	100
L	33	30	15	11	8	3	100
NL	29	37	13	13	6	2	100
A	15	19	19	26	12	10	100
P	9	43	19	3	17	10	100
FIN	9	26	29	28	6	3	100
S	9	18	21	40	7	5	100
UK	12	22	17	36	8	5	100
EU12	20	34	14	17	9	6	100

Source: European Commission services.

TABLE 6-7: The Need For a European Government (Percent by Country)

Question: Do you think that, to make further progress in building Europe, it is necessary or not to have an elected European government?

Countries	Yes, necessary	No, not necessary	Don't know	Total
EU15	54	31	15	100
B	58	26	16	100
DK	13	82	5	100
West D	55	32	13	100
D	55	32	14	100
East D	52	33	15	100
GR	63	24	13	100
E	50	25	25	100
F	58	29	13	100
IRL	60	19	21	100
I	70	12	18	100
L	47	35	18	100
NL	48	47	6	100
A	37	45	18	100
P	41	38	21	100
FIN	47	40	13	100
S	18	70	12	100
UK	47	39	14	100
EU12	55	30	15	100

Source: European Commission services.

TABLE 6-8a: Opinion on Key Current Issues:
A European Government (Percent by Country)

Question: What is your opinion on each of the following proposals?
Please tell me for each proposal, whether you are for it or against it.
The European Union should have a European government responsible
to the European Parliament and to the European Council of Heads of
State and Government.

SPLIT BALLOT A

Countries	For	Against	Don't know	Total
EU15	61	16	23	100
B	59	16	25	100
DK	32	56	12	100
West D	59	19	22	100
D	59	19	22	100
East D	59	19	22	100
GR	65	11	24	100
E	68	8	25	100
F	63	16	21	100
IRL	54	11	35	100
I	69	5	26	100
L	66	17	17	100
NL	76	13	11	100
A	49	23	28	100
P	45	14	41	100
FIN	54	22	24	100
S	42	30	29	100
UK	58	22	21	100
EU12	62	15	23	100

Source: European Commission services.

TABLE 6-8b: Opinion on Key Current Issues:
A European Government (Percent by Country)

Question: What is your opinion on each of the following proposals? Please tell me for each proposal, whether you are for it or against it. The European Union should have a European government responsible to the European Parliament.

SPLIT BALLOT B

Countries	For	Against	Don't know	Total
EU15	59	18	24	100
B	64	13	23	100
DK	29	55	16	100
West D	63	19	17	100
D	63	19	18	100
East D	60	19	21	100
GR	62	12	26	100
E	64	8	28	100
F	61	15	25	100
IRL	50	13	37	100
I	68	5	26	100
L	66	17	17	100
NL	76	13	11	100
A	49	23	28	100
P	45	14	41	100
FIN	54	22	24	100
S	42	30	29	100
UK	58	22	21	100
EU12	62	15	23	100

Source: European Commission services.

TABLE 6-9: The Feeling of Overall Life Satisfaction

Question: On the whole, are you very satisfied, fairly satisfied, not very satisfied, or not at all satisfied with the life you lead?

Only for autumn 1988: All in all, to what extent would you say you are satisfied with the life you lead at this time? Please use this scale (10 points) to decide on your reply. "10" means you are completely satisfied and "1" means you are completely dissatisfied. Autumn 1988 figures are, consequently, not directly comparable. Recoding in this table is as follows: Points 1 and 2 of the scale = not at all satisfied; points 3, 4, 5 = Not very satisfied; points 6, 7, 8 = Fairly satisfied; points 9 and 10 = Very satisfied.

	1973 IX	1975 V-VI	1975 X-XI	1976 V-VI	1976 XI	1977 IV-V	1977 X-XI	1978 V-VI	1978 X-XI	1979 IV
COMMUNITY (EUR 10)*										
	%	%	%	%	%	%	%	%	%	%
Very satisfied	21	20	19	20	20	20	22	22	22	21
Fairly satisfied	58	57	56	55	55	55	57	55	57	56
Not very satisfied	16	16	17	18	18	18	15	16	15	17
Not at all satisfied	4	5	6	6	6	6	5	6	5	5
No reply	1	2	2	1	1	1	1	1	1	1
Total	100	100	100	100	100	100	100	100	100	100
N	13484	9550	9150	8627	9210	9044	8936	9327	8788	8976

TABLE 6-9 (continued)

	1980 IV	1981 IV	1982 III-IV	1982 X	1983 III-IV	1983 X	1984 III-IV	1984 X-XI	1985 III-IV	1985 X-XI
	%	%	%	%	%	%	%	%	%	%
Very satisfied	21	21	24	22	20	18	21	19	23	18
Fairly satisfied	57	55	57	55	59	58	56	60	56	57
Not very satisfied	16	17	14	17	15	16	16	16	15	18
Not at all satisfied	5	6	4	5	5	6	6	4	5	6
No reply	1	1	1	1	1	2	1	1	1	1
Total	100	100	100	100	100	100	100	100	100	100
N	8882	9898	11676	9686	9790	9725	9746	9909	9936	9846

COMMUNITY (EUR 10)*

* Including Greece from April 1981.

69

TABLE 6-9 (continued)

COMMUNITY (EUR 10)*

	1986 III-IV	1986 X-XI	1987 IV	1987 X-XI	1988 III-IV	1988 X-XI	1989 III-IV	1989 VII	1989 X-XI	1990 III-IV
	%	%	%	%	%	%	%	%	%	%
Very satisfied	22	20	22	19	23	20	24	26	25	26
Fairly satisfied	59	58	59	57	59	49	60	56	60	57
Not very satisfied	14	16	14	17	13	25	11	13	11	12
Not at all satisfied	4	5	4	6	4	5	4	4	3	4
No reply	1	1	1	1	1	1	1	1	1	1
Total	100	100	100	100	100	100	100	100	100	100
N	9822	9827	9652	9566	9709	9781	9675	9812	19199	9600

TABLE 6-9 (continued)

	COMMUNITY (EUR 10)*								
	1990 X-XI	1991 III	1991 X-XI	1992 III-IV	1992 IX-X	1993 III-IV	1993 X-XI	1994 IV-V	1994 XII
	%	%	%	%	%	%	%	%	%
Very satisfied	21	26	24	23	24	23	22	22	21
Fairly satisfied	61	59	58	57	57	58	59	59	61
Not very satisfied	12	12	13	14	13	14	15	15	13
Not at all satisfied	5	3	4	5	5	5	4	4	4
No reply	1	0	1	1	1	0	0	0	1
Total	100	100	100	100	100	100	100	100	100
N	9600	9800	9800	9800	9800	9800	9800	9800	9800

* Including Greece from April 1981.

71

TABLE 6-9 (continued)

	1985 X-XI %	1986 III-IV %	1986 X-XI %	1987 IV %	1987 X-XI %	1988 III-IV %	1988 X-XI %	1989 III-IV %	1989 VII %	1989 X-XI %
	COMMUNITY (EUR 12)†									
Very satisfied	18	22	19	23	19	23	20	23	24	24
Fairly satisfied	56	58	57	57	56	58	48	60	57	59
Not very satisfied	19	15	17	15	18	14	26	12	14	13
Not at all satisfied	6	5	6	4	6	4	5	4	4	3
No reply	1	1	1	1	1	1	1	1	1	1
Total	100	100	100	100	100	100	100	100	100	100
N	11849	11831	11837	11651	11583	11731	11794	11678	11819	23199

72

TABLE 6-9 (continued)

	COMMUNITY (EUR 12)†											
	1990 III-IV	1990 X-XI	1991 III	1991 X-XI	1992 III-IV	1992 IX-X	1993 III-IV	1993 X-XI	1994 IV-V	1994 XII
	%	%	%	%	%	%	%	%	%	%
Very satisfied	26	20	24	23	22	23	21	20	20	20
Fairly satisfied	57	61	59	58	58	57	58	59	59	61
Not very satisfied	13	14	13	14	15	14	16	17	16	14
Not at all satisfied	4	5	4	4	4	5	5	4	4	4
No reply	0	0	0	1	1	1	0	0	1	1
Total	100	100	100	100	100	100	100	100	100	100
N	11600	12600	12800	12800	12800	12800	12800	12800	12800	12800

† Including Spain and Portugal. Ex-GDR included from autumn 1990.

Source: European Commission services.

TABLE 6-10: The Feeling of Satisfaction With the Way Democracy Works

Question: On the whole, are you very satisfied, fairly satisfied, not very satisfied, or not at all satisfied with the way democracy works in (*your country*)?

In July 1989, the representative sample of each country was split in two. The usual question was asked to the first sample group; to the second, the following question was asked: "Some people are for the present government of (*your country*). Others are against it. Putting aside whether you are for or against the present government, on the whole, are you very satisfied, fairly satisfied, not very satisfied, or not at all satisfied with the way democracy works in (*your country*)?" As there is no strong difference between the results of the two questions, the data presented have been obtained by summing up the results of both sample groups' responses.

Only for autumn 1988: On the whole, to what extent would you say you are satisfied with the way democracy works in (*your country*)? Answers on a 10 point scale have been recoded as in the previous table.

	1973 IX	1976 XI	1977 IV-V	1977 X-XI	1978 V-VI	1978 X-XI	1979 IV	1979 X	1980 X-XI	1981 X-XI
	%	%	%	%	%	%	%	%	%	%
COMMUNITY (EUR 10)*										
Very satisfied	8	7	7	6	6	6	6	7	7	8
Fairly satisfied	40	42	44	48	49	43	43	44	40	42
Not very satisfied	33	29	28	26	27	30	28	27	30	28
Not at all satisfied	13	16	16	13	12	14	16	15	17	14
No reply	6	6	5	7	6	7	7	7	6	8
Total	100	100	100	100	100	100	100	100	100	100
N	13484	9210	9044	8936	9327	8788	8976	9021	9001	9911

74

TABLE 6-10 (continued)

	1982 III-IV	1982 X	1983 III-IV	1983 X	1984 III-IV	1984 X-XI	1985 III-IV	1985 X-XI	1986 III-IV	1986 X-XI
COMMUNITY (EUR 10)*	%	%	%	%	%	%	%	%	%	%
Very satisfied	8	8	8	8	8	8	8	7	7	8
Fairly satisfied	41	41	41	43	42	43	42	42	47	42
Not very satisfied	30	28	30	28	30	32	31	31	28	30
Not at all satisfied	14	16	15	14	14	13	14	14	12	13
No reply	7	7	6	7	6	4	5	6	6	6
Total	100	100	100	100	100	100	100	100	100	100
N	11676	9689	9790	9725	9746	9909	9936	9846	9822	9827

* Including Greece from October 1980.

75

TABLE 6-10 (continued)

	1987 IV %	1987 X-XI %	1988 III-IV %	1988 X-XI %	1989 III-IV %	1989 VII %	1989 X-XI %	1990 III-IV %	1990 X-XI %	1991 III %
Very satisfied	7	6	8	10	8	9	9	8	9	9
Fairly satisfied	48	44	46	40	48	47	47	47	42	49
Not very satisfied	28	32	30	36	28	27	28	28	29	28
Not at all satisfied	12	14	12	11	12	11	12	13	15	11
No reply	5	4	4	3	4	6	4	4	5	3
Total	100	100	100	100	100	100	100	100	100	100
N	9652	9566	9709	9781	9675	9812	19199	9600	9600	9800

COMMUNITY (EUR 10)*

TABLE 6-10 (continued)

	COMMUNITY (EUR 10)*							
	1991 X-XI	1992 III-IV	1992 X-XI	1993 III-IV	1993 X-XI	1994 IV-V	1994 XII	
	%	%	%	%	%	%	%	
Very satisfied	6	7	6	5	5	5	6	
Fairly satisfied	42	42	39	37	39	40	46	
Not very satisfied	32	32	33	33	34	34	33	
Not at all satisfied	16	15	19	22	19	17	13	
No reply	4	4	3	3	3	4	2	
Total	100	100	100	100	100	100	100	
N	9800	9800	9800	9800	9800	9800	9800	

* Including Greece from October 1980.

77

TABLE 6-10 (continued)

COMMUNITY (EUR 12)†

	1985 X-XI	1986 III-IV	1986 X-XI	1987 IV	1987 X-XI	1988 III-IV	1988 X-XI	1989 III-IV	1989 VII	1989 X-XI
	%	%	%	%	%	%	%	%	%	%
Very satisfied	8	8	10	8	7	8	10	8	9	10
Fairly satisfied	41	45	42	46	44	45	39	48	47	47
Not very satisfied	31	28	29	29	31	30	37	28	27	27
Not at all satisfied	14	12	12	12	13	12	11	12	11	12
No reply	6	7	7	5	5	5	3	4	6	4
Total	100	100	100	100	100	100	100	100	100	100
N	11849	11831	11837	11651	11583	11731	11794	11678	11819	23199

TABLE 6-10 (continued)

COMMUNITY (EUR 12)†

	1990 III-IV	1990 X-XI	1991 III	1991 X-XI	1992 III-IV	1992 IX-X	1993 III-IV	1993 X-XI	1994 IV-V	1994 XII
	%	%	%	%	%	%	%	%	%	%
Very satisfied	9	9	9	7	7	6	5	5	5	5
Fairly satisfied	47	43	48	43	42	39	37	38	39	44
Not very satisfied	28	29	29	32	32	33	34	35	36	35
Not at all satisfied	12	14	11	14	15	18	21	19	17	14
No reply	4	5	3	4	4	4	3	3	3	2
Total	100	100	100	100	100	100	100	100	100	100
N	11600	12600	12800	12800	12800	12800	12800	12800	12800	12800

† Including Spain and Portugal. Ex-GDR included from autumn 1990.

Source: European Commission services.

TABLE 6-11: Basic Attitudes Toward Society

Question: On this card (*show card*) are three basic kinds of attitudes vis-á-vis the society we live in. Please choose the one that best describes your own opinion: 1) The entire way our society is organized must be changed radically by revolutionary action; 2) Our society must be improved gradually by reforms (in 1970, "by intelligent reforms"); 3) Our present society must be defended valiantly against all subversive forces.

	1970 II-III	1976 XI	1977 IV-V	1977 X-XI	1978 V-VI	1978 X-XI	1979 IV	1979 X	1980 X
	%	%	%	%	%	%	%	%	%
Revolutionary action	:	8	8	6	5	7	5	7	6
Reforms	:	60	55	55	55	59	62	57	55
Defense against subversion	:	26	31	32	33	27	26	29	31
No reply	:	6	6	7	7	7	7	7	8
Total	:	100	100	100	100	100	100	100	100
N	:	9210	9044	8936	9327	8788	8976	9021	8882

COMMUNITY (EUR 10)*

TABLE 6-11 (continued)

	COMMUNITY (EUR 10)*								
	1980 X-XI	1981 IV	1981 X-XI	1982 III-IV	1982 X	1983 III-IV	1983 X	1984 III-IV	1984 X-XI
	%	%	%	%	%	%	%	%	%
Revolutionary action	6	7	6	5	5	4	6	4	5
Reforms	57	55	57	59	57	60	60	63	63
Defense against subversion	30	31	29	28	30	30	27	25	26
No reply	7	7	8	8	8	6	7	8	6
Total	100	100	100	100	100	100	100	100	100
N	10001	9898	9911	11676	9689	9790	9725	9746	9909

* Including Greece from October 1980.

TABLE 6-11 (continued)

COMMUNITY (EUR 10)*

	1985 III-IV	1985 X-XI	1986 III-IV	1986 X-XI	1987 IV	1987 X-XI	1988 III-IV	1988 X-XI	1989 III-IV
	%	%	%	%	%	%	%	%	%
Revolutionary action	5	5	5	4	5	4	4	4	4
Reforms	63	63	61	62	62	65	67	67	70
Defense against subversion	26	26	28	28	26	25	24	23	20
No reply	6	6	6	6	7	6	5	6	6
Total	100	100	100	100	100	100	100	100	100
N	9926	9846	9822	9827	9652	9566	9709	9781	9675

TABLE 6-11 (continued)

	COMMUNITY (EUR 10)*		
	1989 X-XI	1990 III-IV	1990 X-XI
	%	%	%
Revolutionary action	5	6	4
Reforms	62	63	65
Defense against subversion	28	27	26
No reply	5	4	5
Total	100	100	100
N	9599	9600	9600

* Including Greece from October 1980.

TABLE 6-11 (continued)

	COMMUNITY (EUR 12)†								
	1985 X-XI	1986 III-IV	1986 X-XI	1987 IV	1987 X-XI	1988 III-IV	1988 X-XI	1989 III-IV	1989 X-XI
	%	%	%	%	%	%	%	%	%
Revolutionary action	5	5	4	4	4	4	4	4	5
Reforms	63	61	63	64	66	68	69	71	63
Defense against subversion	24	25	25	24	22	22	21	19	26
No reply	8	9	8	8	8	6	6	6	6
Total	100	100	100	100	100	100	100	100	100
N	11849	11831	11837	11651	11583	11731	11794	11678	11599

TABLE 6-11 (continued)

	COMMUNITY (EUR 12)†	
	1990 III-IV %	1990 X-XI %
Revolutionary action	6	4
Reforms	65	68
Defense against subversion	24	22
No reply	5	6
Total	100	100
N	11600	12600

† Including Spain and Portugal. Ex-GDR included from autumn 1990.

Source: European Commission services.

TABLE 6-12: Attitudes Toward the Unification of Western Europe

Question: In general, are you for or against efforts being made to unify Western Europe? If *for*, are you very much for this, or only to some extent? If *against*, are you only to some extent against or very much against?

The data for 1952/1967, including June 1962, are from surveys financed by the U.S. Information Agency and, for the following years, as well as February/March 1952, from surveys financed by the Commission of the European Communities. Notwithstanding some differences in the wording, the question was, initially, as follows: "Are you in general for or against making efforts towards uniting Western Europe?" In Great Britain (from 1955 to 1967), in Germany (from February 1955 to April 1956, as well as in June 1962), and in Italy (in 1955 and in 1962), the question specified: ". . . Western Europe, including Great Britain." In 1970, 1973, and 1975, the interviewed individuals were asked whether they were in favor, indifferent, or not in favor of the European unification. Cf.: "L'Opinion publique et l'Europe des Six"; *Sondages*, Paris, n[2]1, 1963, p. 46; "Europeans and European Unification, Brussels, June 1972, pp. 71/72; *Euro-Barometre* n[2]4, December 1975, pp. 54/56.

	COMMUNITY (EUR 10)*									
	1973 IX	1975 V-VI	1975 X	1978 X-XI	1979 IV	1979 X	1980 IV	1980 X-XI	1981 IV	1981 X-XI
	%	%	%	%	%	%	%	%	%	%
For very much	30	35	31	30	30	30	27	29	26	31
For to some extent	33	34	38	45	45	45	46	43	43	43
Against to some extent	6	5	5	8	6	8	9	9	10	9
Against very much	5	4	4	3	4	4	4	4	6	4
No reply	26	22	22	14	15	13	14	15	15	13
Total	100	100	100	100	100	100	100	100	100	100
N	13484	9550	9150	8788	8976	9021	8882	9001	9878	9911

TABLE 6-12 (continued)

COMMUNITY (EUR 10)*

	1982 III-IV	1982 X	1983 III-IV	1983 X	1984 III-IV	1984 X-XI	1985 III-IV	1985 X-XI	1986 III-IV	1986 X-XI
	%	%	%	%	%	%	%	%	%	%
For very much	26	26	29	31	25	30	35	28	32	36
For to some extent	45	44	45	44	46	47	42	47	45	44
Against to some extent	10	10	8	7	10	8	7	9	7	8
Against very much	5	4	3	3	4	3	3	4	3	3
No reply	14	16	15	15	15	12	13	12	13	9
Total	100	100	100	100	100	100	100	100	100	100
N	11676	9689	9790	9725	9746	9909	9936	9846	9822	9827

* Including Greece from October 1980.

87

TABLE 6-12 (continued)

COMMUNITY (EUR 10)*

	1987 IV	1987 X-XI	1988 III-IV	1988 X-XI	1989 III-IV	1989 VII	1989 X-XI	1990 III-IV	1990 X-XI	1991 III
	%	%	%	%	%	%	%	%	%	%
For very much	37	32	26	28	29	29	36	35	32	32
For to some extent	40	46	47	50	50	47	42	45	48	47
Against to some extent	8	8	11	9	9	9	8	8	8	10
Against very much	4	3	4	5	3	3	3	3	3	3
No reply	11	11	12	8	9	12	11	9	9	8
Total	100	100	100	100	100	100	100	100	100	100
N	9652	9566	9706	9781	9675	9812	19199	9600	9600	9800

TABLE 6-12 (continued)

	COMMUNITY (EUR 10)*							
	1991 X-XI	1992 III-IV	1992 IX-X	1992 XI	1993 III-IV	1993 X-XI	1994 XII
	%	%	%	%	%	%	%
For very much	31	28	25	25	25	25	24
For to some extent	47	48	47	46	48	48	49
Against to some extent	9	11	13	14	13	13	12
Against very much	4	5	7	7	6	6	6
No reply	9	8	8	8	8	8	9
Total	100	100	100	100	100	100	100
N	9800	9800	9800	9800	9800	9800	9800

* Including Greece from October 1980.

TABLE 6-12 (continued)

	COMMUNITY (EUR 12)†									
	1985 X-XI	1986 III-IV	1986 X-XI	1987 IV	1987 X-XI	1988 III-IV	1988 X-XI	1989 III-IV	1989 VII	1989 X-XI
	%	%	%	%	%	%	%	%	%	%
For very much	29	33	37	38	33	28	29	30	29	37
For to some extent	45	44	42	39	44	45	49	50	46	41
Against to some extent	9	7	7	7	7	10	8	8	8	7
Against very much	3	2	3	3	3	4	4	3	3	3
No reply	14	14	11	13	13	13	10	9	14	12
Total	100	100	100	100	100	100	100	100	100	100
N	11849	11831	11837	11651	11583	11731	11794	11678	11819	23199

TABLE 6-12 (continued)

	COMMUNITY (EUR 12)†									
	1990 III-IV	1990 X-XI	1991 III	1991 X-XI	1992 III-IV	1992 IX-X	1992 XI	1993 III-IV	1993 X-XI	1994 XII
	%	%	%	%	%	%	%	%	%	%
For very much	36	34	34	33	30	27	26	26	26	24
For to some extent	44	47	47	46	46	46	45	48	47	49
Against to some extent	8	8	8	9	11	13	13	13	12	12
Against very much	3	2	3	3	5	6	7	5	6	6
No reply	9	9	8	9	8	8	9	8	9	9
Total	100	100	100	100	100	100	100	100	100	100
N	11600	12600	12800	12800	12800	12800	12800	12800	12800	12800

† Including Spain and Portugal. Ex-GDR included from autumn 1990.

Source: European Commission services.

TABLE 6-13: Attitudes Toward Membership in the European Community

Question: Generally speaking, do you think that (*your country's*) membership in the European Community (Common Market) is a good thing, a bad thing, or neither good nor bad?

	1973 IX	1974 IV-V	1974 X-XI	1975 V-VI	1975 X	1976 V-VI	1976 XI	1977 IV-V	1977 X-XI
	COMMUNITY (EUR 10)*								
	%	%	%	%	%	%	%	%	%
Good thing	56	59	60	59	63	53	55	57	56
Bad thing	11	14	14	9	9	14	13	14	14
Neither good nor bad	20	18	18	23	21	24	25	21	23
No reply	13	9	8	9	7	9	7	8	7
Total	100	100	100	100	100	100	100	100	100
N	13484	8922	9253	9550	9150	8627	9210	9044	8936

TABLE 6-13 (continued)

COMMUNITY (EUR 10)*

	1978 V-VI %	1978 X-XI %	1979 IV %	1979 VI %	1979 X %	1980 IV %	1980 X-XI %	1981 IV %	1981 X-XI %
Good thing	53	60	59	54	58	55	53	50	53
Bad thing	13	10	12	14	12	15	16	17	14
Neither good nor bad	24	22	21	25	23	22	23	25	26
No reply	10	8	8	8	7	8	8	8	7
Total	100	100	100	100	100	100	100	100	100
N	9327	8788	8976	8126	9021	8882	9001	9898	9911

* Including Greece from October 1980.

TABLE 6-13 (continued)

	COMMUNITY (EUR 10)*									
	1982 III-IV	1982 X	1983 III-IV	1983 X	1984 III-IV	1984 X-XI	1985 III-IV	1985 X-XI	1986 III-IV
	%	%	%	%	%	%	%	%	%
Good thing	52	51	54	55	55	58	57	60	62
Bad thing	14	15	13	13	11	11	12	12	10
Neither good nor bad	26	27	25	24	27	26	24	23	21
No reply	8	7	8	8	7	5	7	5	7
Total	100	100	100	100	100	100	100	100	100
N	1167	9689	9790	9725	9746	9909	9936	9846	9822

TABLE 6-13 (continued)

	COMMUNITY (EUR 10)*										
	1986 X-XI	1987 IV	1987 X-XI	1988 III-IV	1988 X-XI	1989 III-IV	1989 VII	1989 X-XI	1990 III-IV
	%	%	%	%	%	%	%	%	%
Good thing	61	60	65	57	65	64	64	65	65
Bad thing	10	12	9	12	9	9	8	8	9
Neither good nor bad	23	21	20	26	21	22	21	20	20
No reply	6	7	6	5	5	5	7	7	6
Total	100	100	100	100	100	100	100	100	100
N	9827	9652	9566	9709	9781	9675	9812	19199	9600

* Including Greece from October 1980.

95

TABLE 6-13 (continued)

| | COMMUNITY (EUR 10)* | | | | | | | | | | |
	1990 X-XI %	1991 III %	1991 X-XI %	1992 III-IV %	1992 IX-X %	1992 XI %	1993 III-IV %	1993 X-XI %	1994 IV-V %
Good thing	68	70	68	64	60	59	61	57	55
Bad thing	8	7	8	11	12	13	12	13	13
Neither good nor bad	19	18	18	20	22	22	22	25	27
No reply	5	5	6	5	6	6	5	5	5
Total	100	100	100	100	100	100	100	100	100
N	9600	9800	9800	9800	9800	9800	9800	9800	9800

TABLE 6-13 (continued)

	COMMUNITY (EUR 10)*		
	1994 XII		
	%		
Good thing	60		
Bad thing	12		
Neither good nor bad	23		
No reply	5		
Total	100		
N	9800		

* Including Greece from October 1980.

TABLE 6-13 (continued)

	1985 X-XI	1986 III-IV	1986 X-XI	1987 IV	1987 X-XI	1988 III-IV	1988 X-XI	1989 III-IV	1989 VII
	COMMUNITY (EUR 12)†								
	%	%	%	%	%	%	%	%	%
Good thing	60	62	62	60	65	58	66	65	63
Bad thing	11	9	9	11	8	11	8	8	7
Neither good nor bad	22	20	22	21	20	25	21	21	21
No reply	7	9	7	8	7	6	5	6	9
Total	100	100	100	100	100	100	100	100	100
N	11849	11831	11837	11651	11583	11731	11794	11678	11819

TABLE 6-13 (continued)

	COMMUNITY (EUR 12)†								
	1989 X-XI	1990 III-IV	1990 X-XI	1991 III	1991 X-XI	1992 III-IV	1992 IX-X	1992 XI	1993 III-IV
	%	%	%	%	%	%	%	%	%
Good thing	65	65	69	72	69	65	60	58	60
Bad thing	8	8	7	6	8	10	12	13	12
Neither good nor bad	20	21	18	17	17	19	23	24	23
No reply	7	6	6	5	6	6	5	5	5
Total	100	100	100	100	100	100	100	100	100
N	23199	11600	12600	12800	12800	12800	12800	12800	12800

† Including Spain and Portugal. Ex-GDR included from autumn 1990.

TABLE 6-13 (continued)

	COMMUNITY (EUR 12) †		
	1993 X-XI	1994 IV-V	1994 XII
	%	%	%
Good thing	57	54	58
Bad thing	13	13	12
Neither good nor bad	25	28	25
No reply	5	5	5
Total	100	100	100
N	12800	12800	12800

† Including Spain and Portugal. Ex-GDR included from autumn 1990.

Source: European Commission services.

TABLE 6-14: The Feeling That One's Country Has Benefited from Being a Member of the European Union

Question: Taking everything into consideration, would you say that (*your country*) has, on balance, benefited or not from being a member of the European Community (Common Market)?

The figures for 1987-I are taken from the Special 30th Anniversary of the E.E.C. Edition "Europe 2000," Brussels, March 1987, p. A4.

	COMMUNITY (EUR 10)												
	1983 III-IV	1984 III-IV	1984 X-XI	1985 III-IV	1985 X-XI	1986 III-IV	1986 X-XI	1987 I	1987 IV	1987 X-XI
	%	%	%	%	%	%	%	%	%	%
Benefited	52	46	48	50	53	51	55	59	54	59
Not benefited	25	30	34	32	30	27	28	26	28	25
No reply	23	24	18	18	17	22	17	15	18	16
Total	100	100	100	100	100	100	100	100	100	100
N	9790	9746	9909	9936	9846	9822	9827	9926	9652	9566

TABLE 6-14 (continued)

	COMMUNITY (EUR 10)											
	1988 III-IV	1988 X-XI	1989 III-IV	1989 VII	1989 X-XI	1990 III-IV	1990 X-XI	1991 III	1991 X-XI	1992 III-IV
	%	%	%	%	%	%	%	%	%	%
Benefited	56	60	57	55	59	59	59	58	55	54
Not benefited	27	25	26	24	23	24	23	25	26	28
No reply	17	15	17	21	18	17	18	17	19	18
Total	100	100	100	100	100	100	100	100	100	100
N	9709	9781	9675	9812	19199	9600	9600	9800	9800	9800

TABLE 6-14 (continued)

	COMMUNITY (EUR 10)						
	1992 IX-X	1992 XI	1993 III-IV	1993 X-XI	1994 IV-V	1994 XII	
	%	%	%	%	%	%	
Benefited	49	48	48	45	41	50	
Not benefited	33	34	35	35	43	30	
No reply	18	18	17	20	16	20	
Total	100	100	100	100	100	100	
N	9800	9800	9800	9800	9800	9800	

TABLE 6-14 (continued)

	COMMUNITY (EUR 12)*											
	1986 III-IV	1986 X-XI	1987 I	1987 IV	1987 X-XI	1988 III-IV	1988 X-XI	1989 III-IV	1989 VII	1989 X-XI		
	%	%	%	%	%	%	%	%	%	%		
Benefited	46	51	53	49	56	52	56	55	52	59		
Not benefited	32	31	30	33	28	30	28	28	25	22		
No reply	22	18	17	18	16	18	16	17	23	19		
Total	100	100	100	100	100	100	100	100	100	100		
N	11831	11837	11920	11651	11583	11731	11794	11678	11819	23199		

TABLE 6-14 (continued)

	COMMUNITY (EUR 12)*											
	1990 III-IV	1990 X-XI	1991 III	1991 X-XI	1992 II-IV	1992 IX-X	1992 XI	1993 III-IV	1993 X-XI	1994 IV-V
	%	%	%	%	%	%	%	%	%	%
Benefited	59	59	59	56	53	49	49	48	45	47
Not benefited	24	23	24	25	29	33	34	35	35	34
No reply	17	18	17	19	18	18	17	17	20	19
Total	100	100	100	100	100	100	100	100	100	100
N	11600	12600	12800	12800	12800	12800	12800	12800	12800	12800

* Including Spain and Portugal. Ex-GDR included from autumn 1990.

TABLE 6-14 (continued)

	COMMUNITY (EUR 12)*		
	1994 XII		
	%		
Benefited	48		
Not benefited	32		
No reply	20		
Total	100		
N	12800		

* Including Spain and Portugal. Ex-GDR included from autumn 1990.

Source: European Commission services.

TABLE 6-15: Attitudes If the Community Had Been Scrapped

From November 1975: If you were to be told tomorrow that the European Community (Common Market) had been scrapped, would you be. . . . In 1974 and May 1975: If you were to be told tomorrow that (your country) was leaving the Common Market. . . . From 1971 to 1973: If you were to be told tomorrow that the Common Market had been scrapped. . . .

	1973 IX	1974 IV-V	1974 X-XI	1975 V-VI	1975 X	1977 X-XI	1981 IV	1981 X-XI	1982 III-IV	1982 X
	%	%	%	%	%	%	%	%	%	%
Would be very sorry	41	48	49	50	47	45	37	38	40	38
Would be indifferent	36	27	26	30	33	32	36	38	36	36
Would be relieved	10	13	13	9	9	12	16	12	12	15
No reply	13	12	12	11	11	11	11	12	12	11
Total	100	100	100	100	100	100	100	100	100	100
N	13484	8922	9253	9550	9150	8936	9898	9911	11676	9689

COMMUNITY (EUR 10)*

* Including Greece from April 1981.

TABLE 6-15 (continued)

	COMMUNITY (EUR 10)*											
	1983 III-IV	1983 X	1984 III-IV	1984 X-XI	1985 III-IV	1985 X-XI	1986 III-IV	1986 X-XI	1987 IV	1987 X-XI
	%	%	%	%	%	%	%	%	%	%
Would be very sorry	41	40	38	39	41	43	43	41	43	45
Would be indifferent	39	37	39	42	38	37	36	39	37	38
Would be relieved	9	11	10	10	11	10	9	10	9	8
No reply	11	12	13	9	10	10	12	10	11	9
Total	100	100	100	100	100	100	100	100	100	100
N	9790	9725	9746	9909	9936	9846	9822	9827	9652	9566

TABLE 6-15 (continued)

	COMMUNITY (EUR 10)*									
	1988 III-IV	1988 X-XI	1989 III-IV	1989 VII	1989 X-XI	1990 III-IV	1990 X-XI	1991 III	1991 X-XI	1992 III-IV
	%	%	%	%	%	%	%	%	%	%
Would be very sorry	43	43	42	43	48	54	49	49	48	48
Would be indifferent	36	38	38	37	33	37	34	35	33	34
Would be relieved	10	8	9	7	8	9	7	7	8	9
No reply	11	11	11	13	11	10	10	9	11	9
Total	100	100	100	100	100	100	100	100	100	100
N	9709	9781	9675	9812	19199	9600	9600	9800	9800	9800

* Including Greece from April 1981.

109

TABLE 6-15 (continued)

	COMMUNITY (EUR 10)*						
	1992 IX-X	1992 XI	1993 III-IV	1993 X-XI	1994 IV-V	1994 XII
	%	%	%	%	%	%
Would be very sorry	45	43	43	41		43
Would be indifferent	33	36	36	38		37
Would be relieved	13	13	12	12		12
No reply	9	8	9	9		8
Total	100	100	100	100		100
N	9800	9800	9800	9800		9800

* Including Greece from April 1981.

TABLE 6-15 (continued)

	COMMUNITY (EUR 12)†											
	1985 X-XI	1986 III-IV	1986 X-XI	1987 IV	1987 X-XI	1988 III-IV	1988 X-XI	1989 III-IV	1989 VII	1989 X-XI
	%	%	%	%	%	%	%	%	%	%
Would be very sorry	42	42	41	42	45	42	43	43	42	47
Would be indifferent	38	36	39	37	37	36	38	38	37	34
Would be relieved	9	8	9	9	7	10	8	8	7	7
No reply	11	13	11	12	11	12	11	11	14	12
Total	100	100	100	100	100	100	100	100	100	100
N	11849	11831	11837	11651	11583	11731	11794	11678	11819	23199

† Including Spain and Portugal. Ex-GDR included from autumn 1990.

TABLE 6-15 (continued)

	COMMUNITY (EUR 12)†									
	1990 III-IV	1990 X-XI	1991 III	1991 X-XI	1992 III-IV	1992 IX-X	1992 XI	1993 III-IV	1993 X-XI	1994 IV-V
	%	%	%	%	%	%	%	%	%	%
Would be very sorry	48	49	50	49	48	45	42	42	40	
Would be indifferent	34	34	35	33	33	34	38	38	40	
Would be relieved	8	6	6	7	9	12	12	11	11	
No reply	10	11	9	11	10	9	8	9	9	
Total	100	100	100	100	100	100	100	100	100	
N	11600	12600	12800	12800	12800	12800	12800	12800	12800	

TABLE 6-15 (continued)

	COMMUNITY (EUR 12) †			
	1994 XII %			
Would be very sorry	41			
Would be indifferent	38			
Would be relieved	12			
No reply	9			
Total	100			
N	12800			

† Including Spain and Portugal. Ex-GDR included from autumn 1990.

Source: European Commission services.

TABLE 6-16: Impression of the European Parliament As a Result of What Has Been Read or Heard

Question: (If the person has recently seen in the papers, or heard on the radio or TV, anything about the European Parliament, that is, the parliamentary assembly of the EC.) Has what you read or heard given you a generally favorable or unfavorable impression of the European Parliament?

From III-IV 1990, response categories in English are: generally favorable, generally unfavorable and neither favorable nor unfavorable (spontaneous).

	COMMUNITY (EUR 10)										
	1982 X	1983 III-IV	1985 III-IV	1985 X-XI	1986 III-IV	1986 X-XI	1987 III-IV	1987 X-XI	1988 III-IV	1988 X-XI
	%	%	%	%	%	%	%	%	%	%
Rather good	28	35	31	37	39	34	.	42	43	49
Neither good nor bad	26	24	30	28	27	31	.	29	30	28
Rather bad	33	29	33	31	28	29	.	25	22	17
No reply	13	12	6	4	6	6	.	4	5	6
Total	100	100	100	100	100	100	.	100	100	100
N	5252	3579	6067	5278	4754	4184	.	4186	4431	5269

TABLE 6-16 (continued)

	COMMUNITY (EUR 10)									
	1989 III-IV	1989 VII	1989 X-XI	1990 III-IV	1990 X-XI	1991 III	1991 X-XI	1992 III-IV	1992 IX-X	1993 III-IV
	%	%	%	%	%	%	%	%	%	%
Rather good	46	45	54	53	52	52	49	50	45	41
Neither good nor bad	28	29	23	26	25	21	25	23	26	25
Rather bad	21	21	18	15	18	21	20	20	23	29
No reply	5	5	5	6	5	6	6	7	6	5
Total	100	100	100	100	100	100	100	100	100	100
N	5267	6852	5246	4948	4608	4208	4981	4161	5400	4344

TABLE 6-16 (continued)

	COMMUNITY (EUR 12)†											
	1986 III-IV	1986 X-XI	1987 III-IV	1987 X-XI	1988 III-IV	1988 X-XI	1989 III-IV	1989 VII	1989 X-XI	1990 III-IV
	%	%	%	%	%	%	%	%	%	%
Rather good	40	36	34	46	44	50	49	45	54	54
Neither good nor bad	27	31	30	28	31	29	28	29	24	27
Rather bad	25	26	*	22	20	16	18	20	16	14
No reply	8	7	6	4	5	5	5	6	6	5
Total	100	100	100	100	100	100	100	100	100	100
N	5877	5065	5066	5272	5494	6409	6563	8253	6412	6038

* Data not available

116

TABLE 6-16 (continued)

	COMMUNITY (EUR 12)†					
	1990 X-XI	1991 III	1991 X-XI	1992 III-IV	1992 IX-X	1993 III-IV
	%	%	%	%	%	%
Rather good	53	53	50	53	46	42
Neither good nor bad	26	23	27	24	27	22
Rather bad	15	18	17	17	21	31
No reply	6	6	6	6	6	5
Total	100	100	100	100	100	100
N	6159	5614	6613	5588	7072	5796

† Including Spain and Portugal. Ex-GDR included from autumn 1990.

Source: European Commission services.

TABLE 6-17: Importance of the European Parliament's Present Role in the Life of the European Community*

Question: How important, would you say, is the European Parliament in the life of the European Community nowadays?

From III-IV 1990, response categories in English are: very important, important, not very important, not at all important.

	1977 IV-V	1983 III-IV	1984 III-IV	1984 X-XI	1985 III-IV	1985 X-XI	1986 III-IV	1986 X-XI	1987 III-IV	1987 X-XI
	COMMUNITY (EUR 10)*									
	%	%	%	%	%	%	%	%	%	%
Very important	10	11	9	11	12	12	13	10	14	11
Important	27	40	34	39	40	38	40	39	41	42
Not very important	29	27	31	34	28	30	26	29	25	27
Not at all important	10	5	7	7	6	7	5	7	6	6
No reply	24	17	19	9	14	17	16	15	14	14
Index †	2.49	2.69	2.55	2.58	2.67	2.63	2.71	2.63	2.74	2.68

TABLE 6-17 (continued)

	1988 III-IV	1988 X-XI	1989 III-IV	1989 X-XI	1990 III-IV	1990 X-XI	1991 III	1991 X-XI	1992 III-IV	1992 IX-X
	%	%	%	%	%	%	%	%	%	%
Very important	10	12	13	14	16	12	12	12	11	11
Important	41	42	39	45	43	45	42	42	43	43
Not very important	28	26	27	24	23	24	27	25	24	25
Not at all important	6	5	5	4	4	5	5	4	5	4
No reply	15	15	16	13	14	14	15	17	17	17
Index†	2.65	2.73	2.71	2.80	2.83	2.80	2.70	2.75	2.73	2.72

COMMUNITY (EUR 10)*

† Calculated by applying the coefficients 4, 3, 2, and 1 respectively to the various answer codes; the "don't know" categories are excluded from the calculation. The midpoint corresponds to 2.5.
* Including Greece from March–April 1983.

119

TABLE 6-17 (continued)

	COMMUNITY (EUR 10)*	
	1993 III-IV	1994 XII
	%	%
Very important	13	12
Important	44	46
Not very important	24	20
Not at all important	4	4
No reply	15	18
Index †	2.78	2.82

TABLE 6-17 (continued)

	COMMUNITY (EUR 12)**											
	1986 III-IV	1986 X-XI	1987 III-IV	1987 X-XI	1988 III-IV	1988 X-XI	1989 III-IV	1989 X-XI	1990 III-IV	1990 X-XI
	%	%	%	%	%	%	%	%	%	%
Very important	14	11	16	13	11	13	13	15	17	13
Important	38	38	40	41	41	42	40	44	43	45
Not very important	24	26	23	25	25	24	25	23	22	22
Not at all important	5	6	5	5	6	4	5	4	4	4
No reply	19	19	16	16	17	17	17	14	14	16
Index†	2.76	2.68	2.79	2.74	2.69	2.76	2.75	2.81	2.85	2.80

† Calculated by applying the coefficients 4, 3, 2, and 1 respectively to the various answer codes; the "don't know" categories are excluded from the calculation. The midpoint corresponds to 2.5.

** Including Spain and Portugal. Ex-GDR included from autumn 1990.

TABLE 6-17 (continued)

	COMMUNITY (EUR 12)**						
	1991 III	1991 X-XI	1992 III-IV	1992 IX-X	1993 III-IV	1994 XII
	%	%	%	%	%	%
Very important	13	13	12	11	13	12
Important	43	43	43	43	44	47
Not very important	25	23	23	23	23	19
Not at all important	4	4	4	5	4	4
No reply	15	17	18	18	16	19
Index †	2.80	2.79	2.77	2.74	2.79	2.83

* Including Greece from March–April 1983.

† Calculated by applying the coefficients 4, 3, 2, and 1 respectively to the various answer codes; the "don't know" categories are excluded from the calculation. The midpoint corresponds to 2.5.

** Including Spain and Portugal. Ex-GDR included from autumn 1990.

Source: European Commission services.

TABLE 6-18: Desired Future Role for the European Parliament*

Question: Would you, personally, prefer that the European Parliament played a more or a less important part than it does now?

From III-IV 1990, response categories in English are: more important, less important, about the same (spontaneous).

	1983 IV	1983 X	1984 III-IV	1984 X-XI	1985 III-IV	1985 X-XI	1986 III-IV	1986 X-XI	1987 III-IV	1987 X-XI
	COMMUNITY (EUR 10)									
	%	%	%	%	%	%	%	%	%	%
More important role	52	59	50	60	56	56	53	53	48	51
Same role	16	13	17	16	18	15	16	20	18	20
Less important role	10	10	10	10	10	12	12	9	13	11
No reply	22	18	23	14	16	17	19	18	21	18

* Volunteered answer.

TABLE 6-18 (continued)

COMMUNITY (EUR 10)

	1988 III-IV %	1988 X-XI %	1989 III-IV %	1989 X-XI %	1990 III-IV %	1990 X-XI %	1991 III %	1991 X-XI %	1992 III-IV %	1992 IX-X %
More important role	50	44	49	53	52	54	61	58	55	54
Same role	20	25	20	19	19	17	14	16	17	16
Less important role	10	11	10	11	10	10	9	9	10	12
No reply	20	20	21	17	19	19	16	17	18	18

COMMUNITY (EUR 10)

	1993 III-IV %	1994 XII %
More important role	49	48
Same role	20	10
Less important role	13	21
No reply	18	21

TABLE 6-18 (continued)

	COMMUNITY (EUR 12)†									
	1986 III-IV	1986 X-XI	1987 III-IV	1987 X-XI	1988 III-IV	1988 X-XI	1989 III-IV	1989 X-XI	1990 III-IV	1990 X-XI
	%	%	%	%	%	%	%	%	%	%
More important role	50	51	47	50	49	44	49	52	52	53
Same role	16	19	18	19	20	25	20	20	19	17
Less important role	10	8	12	10	9	10	9	10	9	9
No reply	24	22	23	21	22	21	22	18	20	21

† Including Spain and Portugal. Ex-GDR included from autumn 1990.

TABLE 6-18 (continued)

	COMMUNITY (EUR 12)†						
	1991 III	1991 X-XI	1992 III-IV	1992 IX-X	1993 III-IV	1994 XII
	%	%	%	%	%	%
More important role	62	58	56	55	50	48
Same role	15	16	16	16	20	9
Less important role	8	8	9	11	12	22
No reply	16	18	19	18	18	22

† Including Spain and Portugal. Ex-GDR included from autumn 1990.

Source: European Commission services.

TABLE 6-19: Attitudes Toward a Future European Government Responsible to the European Parliament

Question: From October–November 1989, are you for or against the formation of a European Union, with a European government responsible to the European Parliament?

October–November 1988 and March–April 1989, are you for or against the formation, by 1992, of a European government responsible to the European Parliament?

October–November 1987 and March–April 1988, are you for or against the formation of a European government responsible to the European Parliament?

Community (EUR 10)	1987 X-XI	1988 III-IV	1988 X-XI	1989 III-IV	1989 X-XI	1990 III-IV	1990 X-XI
For	49	49	53	55	54	53	54
Against	26	26	22	19	21	22	20
No reply	25	25	25	26	25	25	26
Total	100	100	100	100	100	100	100
N	9566	9709	9781	9675	9599	9600	9600

TABLE 6-19 (continued)

Community (EUR 10)	1991 II	1991 X-XI	1992 III-IV	1992 IX-X	1993 III-IV	1993 X-XI	1994 IV-V
For	58	55	54	50	47	46	50
Against	20	22	21	29	29	28	27
No reply	22	23	25	21	24	26	23
Total	100	100	100	100	100	100	100
N	9800	9800	9800	9800	9800	9800	9800

Community (EUR 10)	1994 XII
For	55
Against	21
No reply	24
Total	100
N	9800

TABLE 6-19 (continued)

Community (EUR 12)*	1987 X-XI	1988 III-IV	1988 X-XI	1989 III-IV	1989 X-XI	1990 III-IV	1990 X-XI
For	48	49	53	55	54	55	55
Against	24	24	20	17	20	21	19
No reply	28	27	27	28	26	24	26
Total	100	100	100	100	100	100	100
N	11583	11731	11794	11678	11599	11600	12600

Community (EUR 12)*	1991 III	1991 X-XI	1992 III-IV	1992 IX-X	1993 III-IV	1993 X-XI	1994 IV-V
For	59	56	55	51	48	47	50
Against	19	20	20	28	27	27	26
No reply	22	24	25	21	25	26	24
Total	100	100	100	100	100	100	100
N	12800	12800	12800	12800	12800	12800	12800

* Ex-GDR included from autumn 1990.

TABLE 6-19 (continued)

Community (EUR 10)	1994 XII
For	55
Against	20
No reply	25
Total	100
N	12800

* Ex-GDR included from autumn 1990.

Source: European Commission services.

Figure 6-1: Expectations As to the Economy: Next Twelve Months

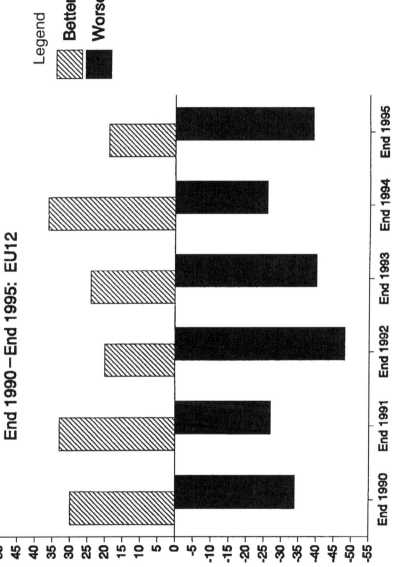

End 1990–End 1995: EU12

Legend
Better
Worse

End 1990   End 1991   End 1992   End 1993   End 1994   End 1995

Source: European Commission services.

Figure 6-2: Support for European Union Membership
1981 to 1995 EU15*

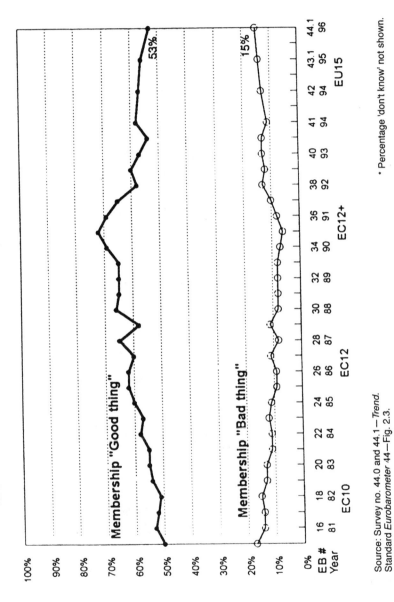

Source: Survey no. 44.0 and 44.1 – *Trend.*
Standard *Eurobarometer* 44 – Fig. 2.3.

* Percentage 'don't know' not shown.

Source: European Commission services.

132

Figure 6-3: Benefit from European Union Membership
1984 to 1995 EU12/EU15†

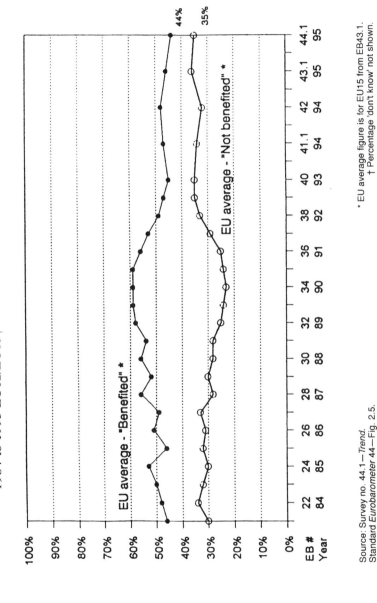

Source: Survey no. 44.1—*Trend*.
Standard *Eurobarometer* 44—Fig. 2.5.

Source: European Commission services.

* EU average figure is for EU15 from EB43.1.
† Percentage 'don't know' not shown.

Figure 6-4: Benefit from European Union Membership, by Country and EU15

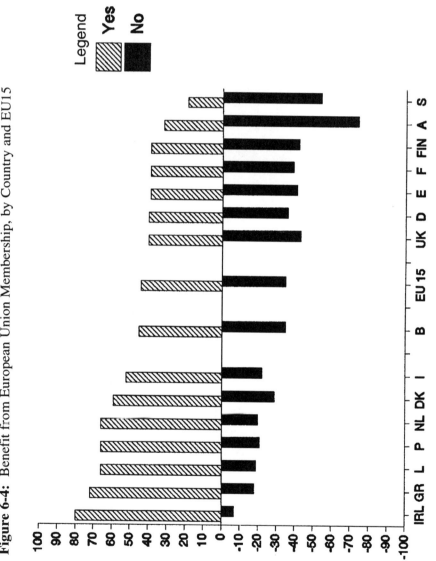

Source: European Commission services.

7 THE EU COMMON FOREIGN AND SECURITY POLICY: CONTRIBUTOR TO THE INTEGRATION PROCESS?

The Treaty of Maastricht, in Articles J to J11, has established a common foreign and security policy for the EU member states. This step is a continuation of Article 30 of the Single European Act of 1987, which provided the legal basis for European Political Cooperation (EPC) in the field of foreign policy and laid the groundwork for close cooperation on questions of European security, which in turn would enhance the development of a European identity in external policy matters (Section 6). Nothing in Article 30 should impede closer cooperation of the EU member states within the framework of the Western European Union (WEU) or the Atlantic Alliance.

The evolution of the EU foreign policy coordination process differs from the common security policy development; the former has been practiced through EPC for more than 25 years, while there has been much talk about a common security policy but so far little has been accomplished in creating an appropriate structure within the EU. Consequently, we will first concentrate on EPC and common foreign policies, and in a subsequent section of this chapter we will focus on common security policy.

EU FOREIGN POLICY COORDINATION MEANS AND PROBLEMS

Key to the coordination process on foreign policy are the political directors of the EU members' foreign policy departments (the heads of the political departments in these ministries). They constitute the Political Committee, which is to meet at least each quarter but may meet more frequently depending on critical foreign policy developments. If necessary, it can convene a meeting of EU foreign ministers within 48 hours at the request of individual EU member states. It also prepares the discussions of ministerial meetings and maintains the continuity of EPC. Specialized working groups can be convened or directed by the Political Committee. A secretariat based in Brussels assists the EU presidency, which changes every six months, in preparing and implementing the activities of the EPC and in administrative matters. The implementation of EPC proposals is also monitored by a European Correspondents Group, which helps the presidency with solving organizational problems.

The Commission is to be fully associated with the work carried out in the common foreign policy field, but it is the Council of Ministers that makes the basic decisions on common policy content and implementation. The president of the Council of Ministers needs to consult the European Parliament on the main aspects and the basic choices of the common foreign policy in question and shall ensure that the views of the EP are taken into consideration (Article J.7 of the Maastricht Treaty). The Council must also decide whether policy implementation costs are charged to the EU budget or to one or more member states (Article J-11).

Decisions by the Council of Ministers on EU foreign policy matters are made by unanimity except for procedural questions and specific issues when the Council authorizes decisions by a qualified majority. The Council also must define common priorities for EU foreign policy and ensure that their combined influence is exerted as effectively as possible by means of concerted and convergent actions. This includes the coordination of EU governments' actions in international organizations and international conferences (Articles J.2 and J.3 provide details of the procedure).

EPC HISTORY AND OPERATIONS

The EPC began its activities following the summit meeting of December 1969 in the Hague, when efforts were initiated to find new ways for the construction of an enlarged community. One of these efforts was the creation of a committee composed of high foreign ministry officials of the "Six" under the chairmanship of Vicomte Etienne Davignon of the Belgian foreign ministry; this later became the Political Committee. This group held a number of sessions beginning in April 1970. The results of the deliberations of the Davignon committee were published in April

1970, in a report of the foreign ministers of the Community member states. In accordance with this report, the foreign ministers began to schedule joint meetings every six months. In important cases the foreign ministers could also call a conference of chiefs of state and government when crucial issues justified such a meeting.[1]

The emergence of the Political Committee as an important factor in the formulation of common foreign policies may pit three organizational and bureaucratic groups against each other. One group consists of the officials of the foreign ministries operating through the Political Committee and, more recently, through a permanent secretariat, which will be concerned with the coordination of a wide range of foreign policy issues and may invade the competencies of the EU structure. Secondly, we have the EU decision-making process, with its own group of civil servants striving to produce and implement external policies in accordance with the provisions of the Community and EU Treaties. It is noteworthy that in this process, which originally was to be dominated by the international civil service of the European Community, we find expanding control by a third group of national officials. These officials operate through the offices of the Permanent Representatives (COREPER), who have an increasingly influential role in the decision-making process of the EU. Some of these national officials come from the foreign ministries of the member states, and others are assigned by the ministries of economics, agriculture, and finance as technical experts. These experts may be called upon to give advice not only to working groups of COREPER, but also to those of the Commission, since the major competencies of the Community are concentrated on the activities with which these technical experts are concerned. Hence, these national officials play perhaps a more salient part in evolving decisions for the EU than do their colleagues of the foreign ministries. Therefore, not only do we see a subversion of the original concepts of Community decision making in the field of foreign policy by the national officials, but we can also discern competition and interpenetration between two distinct national bureaucratic groups struggling, perhaps subtly, to extend their own competencies and those of their institutions.

With such a large number of national officials rubbing elbows with Eurocrats in the numerous working groups set up by the Commission and within COREPER, the question of gradual political socialization inclining the national civil servants involved in these activities toward pro-Community and pro-integration attitudes has been raised frequently and often answered in the affirmative. However, getting to know the Community and integration is not the same thing as getting to love them.

While common experiences in working groups composed of Community and national civil servants may have engendered some attitude shifts among the latter, they did not undirectionally impel integrative attitudes. Indeed, there may be a slow renationalization in the attitudes of the Eurocracy, whose commitment as specified in the EC Treaties should be exclusively the promotion of the Community interests. Some of the ministries in the new member states seem to consider EU civil servants of their nationality as agents to bargain for national advantages.

Since 1969 various summit meetings of the heads of state and government became concerned with foreign policy coordination for the Community member states. In the Hague Summit in 1969, the Council of Foreign Ministers (CFM) was asked to report on ways to achieve political union. In response, the CFM at the Summit in Luxembourg in 1970 asked member governments to engage in consultation on all major foreign policy questions in an intergovernmental framework outside the formal 1957 Rome Treaty Framework, and to meet biannually under the chair of the Council presidency, which rotates biannually among member states.

In 1972, at the Paris Summit, the Commission was given a role in EPC, with close contact to be maintained between EPC and EC bodies to assure a significant position for the EU in world affairs. The achievement of this objective by the 1973 Copenhagen Summit, which also accepted Commission attendance at all EPC meetings, required the CFM to meet quarterly and the Political Committee to meet as frequently as work necessitated, and that the two groups set up essential working parties from the national foreign and other ministries to consider matters together and exchange information.[2]

In 1974 the Paris Summit created a new body, the European Council, whose members would meet triannually, overseeing both the Community and EPC, and whose meetings would be attended by the Commission and the CFM. In 1981 a major initiative by German foreign minister Genscher and Italian foreign minister Colombo was presented 1) to formalize EPC into a new treaty, 2) to increase majority voting opportunities in the Council of Ministers, and 3) to encourage member governments to use their vetoes only in exceptional cases. Although the proposal was not accepted, it contained ideas and served to focus attention on the need to reform EC decision-making procedures. Also in 1981, in a London Summit, a new system of continuity of decision making was introduced, authorizing the immediately preceding and succeeding presidencies to serve in a troika fashion, thus providing more continuity, given the short, six-month presidential terms.[3] Much of this progress has been codified in Article 30 of the Single European Act of 1987 and is further being refined by the Treaty of Maastricht and, hopefully, by the 1996–97 Intergovernmental Conference.

Communications within EPC are excellent and sophisticated. A common telex system, called COREU, has been established to connect the EU member states, and over a hundred communications are transmitted every week. An emergency meeting of the CFM can be set up at very short notice. The steady flow of information and constant exchange of views among the member states have led to a routine that is described as "coordination reflex." As a result of this reflex, the foreign policy of the other members has become more transparent and predictable, and the number of surprising changes of position has decreased. Moreover, in cases of open disagreement this mechanism produces an internal group pressure for adjustments of divergent positions.

Information and consultation, which lead to an effective coordination reflex, are necessary but not sufficient instruments for a full harmonization of views or policies. Common views on some aspects of an issue do not necessarily mean agreement in concrete diplomatic work or on all diplomatic points. Nevertheless, EPC activities are useful in helping to bring about understanding and agreement among the foreign ministries and the top leadership of the EU.[4] Aiding this process is the custom of EU diplomatic representatives in third countries and in international organizations to consult regularly in order to coordinate their positions and actions. This is a very important activity and enlarges further the circle of consultants in the foreign policy process.

EU TREATY LEGAL BASES FOR FOREIGN POLICY ACTIONS

Two issue areas that have been covered in the Treaties dealing with the ESCS, EEC, and EURATOM are common commercial policy and relations with intergovernmental organizations (IGOs). The Commission must submit proposals to the Council of Ministers about the state or states of international organizations with which one or more trade agreements are to be negotiated. These negotiations are to be conducted in consultation with a special committee appointed by the Council and within the framework of such directives as the Council may issue to the committee (Article 113).[5] Decision making by the Council in such a case will be by qualified majority vote.

For relation with intergovernmental organizations—there are global and regional IGOs—common policy positions by EU members are also essential for foreign policy. If all EU members are also participants of the IGO toward which particular policy is being considered, diplomatic representatives of the EU can discuss at the headquarters of the IGO the issues and favorable results that may be anticipated from demarches. For example, such a meeting could take place at United Nations headquarters in New York if the issue dealt with the United Nations. But problems may also arise with some of the regional IGOs, and in that case not all EU member states may be involved.

Finally, EU relations with Third World countries deserve special mention in the area of foreign policy development. An important aspect of these relations was the introduction of association policies that provided preferential treatment of the associate country through the elimination or reduction of tariffs for goods shipped from the associates to the Community, and in many cases also by the grant of financial aid. In return, the associate countries offer certain tariff preferences, called "reverse preferences," for the import of Community products.[6]

The first EC association agreement with 18 Third World countries was signed in 1963 in Yaounde, Cameroon, and was called the Convention of Yaounde. The bulk of the associated countries were former French colonies that had been given some Community advantages before they became independent. A second association agreement was negotiated in the second half of the 1960s with former British possessions (Kenya, Tanzania, Uganda) and was to become the Association of Arusha. However, the impending EC membership of Great Britain changed plans and led to the Convention of Lomé, which was signed in 1990 but was given a ten-year duration. In 1995 there was a mid-term review and the number of ACP (African, Caribbean, and Pacific) states had reached 70. Their European partners were 15 EU states.

Much of the cooperation stimulated by the Lomé Convention is financial, and in 1995 the financial supports offered by the EU and accepted by the ACP amounted to 14.6 billion ECU. But there is also a political side of the cooperation. EU Council of Ministers and ACP Ministers meetings may take place jointly, which can produce better understanding of problems faced and solutions pursued. With crucial votes in the U.N. General Assembly depending at times on elusive majorities, the voting decisions of ACP members may play important roles for the EU. In addition, parliamentarians of ACP countries and in the EU may schedule joint meetings to learn more about political issues they face.[7]

COMMISSION ORGANIZATIONAL FRAMEWORK FOR FOREIGN POLICY

As indicated in Table 7-1, the proposals for the formulation of the Commission's foreign and commercial policy are worked up in Directorate-General I (DG-1), which has been given the main responsibility for the conduct of external relations. Other foreign policy proposals come from Directorate-General VIII (DG-8), concerned primarily with relations to developing countries. The personnel of DG-1 also maintain the daily contacts with the members of the various diplomatic missions accredited to the EU. These contacts provide much of the information needed to formulate and implement policy and to keep the Council of Ministers apprised of all important communications by third country diplomats, of whom more than 90 have been established in Brussels.[8]

As for EPC matters, the Commission has established a new Directorate-General for External Political Relations—DG-1A. Joint actions have been adopted by the EU in accordance with Article J-3 of the Maastricht Treaty regarding former Yugoslavia (eight actions), Russia's parliamentary elections, South Africa, Stability and Growth Pact, anti-personnel unions, Middle East peace process, nonproliferation, and control of dual-use goods.[9] But despite these more recent joint actions, which often depend on EU declarations, foreign policy formulation and implementation have not moved forward as the potential indicated in Article J of the Maastricht Treaty. The emphasis on unanimous voting, even where the Treaty allows qualified voting, is one of the problems of foreign policy and one of the reasons why it has been frequently ineffective. Moreover, because of unanimous voting, as well as the tendency to use declarations as foreign policy means as much as possible, effective EU foreign policy progress has been very limited.[10]

SECURITY ASPECTS

The pursuit of security for the European Union is stipulated in the same article of the Maastricht Treaty as the concern with the common foreign policy (Article J.1). The objective is "to safeguard the common values, fundamental interests and independence of the Union" and "to strengthen the security of the Union and its Member States in all ways." The principles of the U.N. Charter and the Helsinki Final Act as modified by the Paris Charter of 1990 are to be guides for instituting the security policy. The assurance of security may require more than declarations or interstate agreements; the availability and perhaps the application of military force may be necessary. During the last ten years, interest has been expressed in making the Western European Union (WEU) an eventual framework for amassing military security, but despite the fact that the secretariat of the WEU moved to Brussels in the early 1990s, it now contains a planning cell, and even though its permanent Council meets weekly, the connection between the WEU and the EU remains uncertain. The WEU would like to be considered the "European pillar" of NATO, but this can become realistic only if the necessary personnel and logistical assets can be developed by 1998—when WEU is to reach the end of its existence. The earlier hope of the EC and the WEU to develop the latter as the military arm of the Community by 1996 has not been fulfilled. Willem van Eckelen, a former secretary general of the WEU, proposed a comprehensive blueprint in 1991 for the evolution of this organization and regarding its relationship with the Community, with NATO, as well as with the Organization on Security and Cooperation in Europe (OSCE).[11] The current secretary general of the WEU, José Ciutileiro, does not seem to have the same enthusiasm for developing WEU as the main security structure for the EU as his predecessor.

To produce a definitive tie between the EU and the Western European Union on an effective level would require the involvement of the top military staff of the member states in the planning and operational activities of WEU. This may necessitate the establishment of another directorate general or the expansion of DG-1. Meanwhile, not all EU members are also WEU partners: Denmark, Greece, and Ireland are at present outside the WEU, although Greece seems to be willing to join. The so-called "neutrals," Austria, Finland, Sweden, and Ireland, have signaled that they are willing to incorporate peacekeeping, armed humanitarian aid, and crisis management in a revision of the Maastricht Treaty, possibly during the IGC negotiations that were not very successful under the leadership of Ireland and the Netherlands but may improve when Luxembourg is in the chair at the end of 1997.[12]

In May of 1996 some of the problems mentioned above were discussed at a meeting of Council Ministers of the WEU in Birmingham, England, and a declaration was adopted that marks WEU progress on operational and institutional matters. It was recognized that WEU, as both the defense component of the European Union and as a means to strengthen the European pillar of the NATO alliance, has a pivotal role to play in accordance with the agreements reached in Maastricht in 1991 and with the NATO Summit declaration of 1994, in particular by providing the politico-military center of European operations.[13]

In accordance with the Birmingham declaration, closer institutional and operational links with the EU are needed to enhance WEU's capacity to respond to the need to elaborate and implement effectively the decisions.and actions of the Union that have defense implications, in particular those requiring military means and expertise. Combined Joint Trade Forces (CJTF) with NATO may provide bases for European operations that would strengthen WEU's operational capacity and command management. The final aim should be to make further progress toward defining and organizing a European security architecture that meets the needs for stability of the European constituents.[14] The further development of the European Security and Defense Identity was considered as essential by the Birmingham conference, and it was recommended that this could be furthered by including this concern in the deliberations of the IGC.[15]

The Dayton agreement of 1995 regarding Bosnia was considered an essential step for regional peace in former Yugoslavia, although—despite the election in 1996 to initiate a new constitutional system—an optimistic final outcome in political and military terms remains somewhat doubtful.

This development also requires consideration of the "Euro-Corps," consisting mainly of about 35,000 German and French military forces, with limited possible future additions of Belgian and Spanish troops if they could be placed under the political authority of the WEU. How this military organization may be affected by the French government's announcement in the summer of 1996 that it intended to reduce the size of its armed forces requires additional information.

The relationship between WEU and NATO also impacts the future security policy of the Union. Obviously, the experienced NATO command and logistics structure may provide important opportunities for exercising WEU's security responsibilities in Europe. At a meeting in June 1996, following strong pressure from the French government, agreement was reached by the NATO members and EU participants that would identify headquarters and command structures within NATO to be used for "European-only" operations. This may not provide WEU and the EU members with a military carte blanche, but it is a step forward for initiating a Union common security policy while structural and organizational means are being built.[16] France also continues to urge the appointment of a European deputy to the U.S. general commanding NATO, but the success of this move is doubtful.

In the meantime, NATO policy seeks to enlarge eastward and it is hoped that Poland, Hungary, and the Czech Republic become new NATO members. Russia basically opposes this movement for its own security reasons, but the American and West European NATO members seem to support fully NATO's expansion to the east—although it may be a costly undertaking in financial and political terms. Moreover, the Organization for Security and Cooperation in Europe (OSCE), encompassing all European countries, the United States, and Canada, seeks to ensure security in the EU area and, beyond that, a measure of stability. While there was a great deal of enthusiasm when the institutional details were set up at the beginning of the 1990s, it is recognized now that the operational capabilities of OSCE are quite limited.[17]

CONCLUSION

Although the section of the Maastricht Treaty dealing with the common foreign and security policy does not distinguish the current status of accomplishment between the foreign and security policies, it is obvious that the foreign policy section has developed an appropriate framework for intensive research and analysis with the necessary, fairly extensive staffing. The security section has accomplished very little beyond the former WEU secretary-general's blueprint for action and the NATO agreement for limited military resources described earlier.

The problems of the defense policy sector were caused not only by the lack of appropriate institutional preparations but also by the reluctance of WEU to apply the necessary force against the Bosnian Serbs to stop their military build-up and to ensure the protection of non-Serbs against ethnic cleansing and other cruelties. Having the WEU forces bomb and otherwise attack factories turning out military materials and Serb troop assembly points may have slowed down or even stopped Serb attacks, but such activities were limited. And WEU and EU morale was badly hurt by these nonactions in the military field, which, in turn, negatively affected public support for integration.

The Euro-Corps, which had its beginning in the 1990 establishment of a French-German joint brigade encompassing about 4,000 French and German soldiers,[18] will require extensive administrative and logistic work, and progress on this task at present is uncertain.

Considering that the implementation of the common foreign and security policy in the Maastricht Treaty is a very important aspect of the EU, the lack of comprehensive and effective decision making in this issue area is disappointing, especially in the security field where little progress has been made. The loss in terms of impact and identity on the international scene is considerable, and the cost in public opinion very high.

NOTES

[1]For details see "Report of Foreign Ministers" in "Bericht der Aussenminister der Mitgliedstaaten der Europäischen Germeinschaften an die Staats-bzw. Regierungschefs vom 20. Juli 1970, betr. mögliche Fortschritte auf dem Gebiet der politischen Einigung," *Europa Archiv* 25, no. 22 (1970), D520-D524.

[2]For further details see Roy H. Ginsburg, *Foreign Policy Actions of the European Community* (Boulder, CO: Lynne Rienner Publishers, 1989), pp. 45–51.

[3]Ibid.

[4]Wolfgang Wessels, "New Forms of Foreign Policy Formulation in Western Europe," in *Western Europe's Global Reach*, ed. Werner J. Feld (New York: Pergamon Press), pp. 12–29 on pp. 14–20.

[5]This is the new wording of Article 113 as provided in the Maastricht Treaty.

[6]See Werner J. Feld, *The European Community in World Affairs* (New York: Alfred Publishing Co., 1976), pp. 26–29.

[7]Ibid, pp. 122-131, and *The Courier*, no. 155, January-February 1996, "Special Issue on the Revised Lomé Convention."

[8]See Table 7-1 for organizational breakdowns of DG-1 and DG-8.

[9]The Commission Report for the Reflection Group, Annex 17, *Intergovernmental Conference 1996*. For an overall evaluation of EPC and foreign policy actions see Ginsberg, *Foreign Policy Actions*, pp. 165–86.

[10]Ibid.

[11]Main excerpts are found in Werner J. Feld, *The Future of European Security and Defense Policy* (Boulder, CO: Lynne Rienner Publishers, 1992), pp. 85–87.

[12]Ibid., pp. 73–82, and *Financial Times*, 23 July, 1996, p. 2, provide details.

[13]*European Agence International*, Europe Documents no. 96, 10 May, 1996, p. 1.

[14]Ibid., p. 2.

[15]Ibid., p. 4. See also French and British attitudes on strengthening WEU in *Financial Times*, 8 May, 1996, pp. 2, 3, 14.

[16]For details see *Financial Times*, 4 June, 1996, p. 1.

[17]See Giancarlo Aragona, "Lisbon and Beyond: The OSCE in an Emerging European Security Structure," *NATO Review*, (March 1997), pp. 7–10.

[18]For details see Feld, *Future of European Security*, pp. 102–5.

TABLE 7-1: Commission Structure for External Affairs

Directorate-General I	**External Relations:**	**Trade policy, relations with North America, Far East, Australia, and New Zealand.**
Directorate-General IA	**External Relations:**	**Europe and newly independent states, Common Foreign and Security Policy, External Missions.**
Directorate-General VIII	**Development Policy:**	**Management of instruments, finance, West and Central Africa, East and Southern Africa, Caribbean, Pacific and Indian Ocean.**

Source: European Commission services.

8   CONCLUSION AND
THE FUTURE

The regional integration of the European Union faces many obstacles, generally resulting from attachments to nationalism by citizens of many member states and opposition to a federal governmental system. Nevertheless, given the appropriate leadership in some of the EU member states, more and more EU member state citizens may begin to realize the advantages flowing from an appropriate and effective governmental system, a tighter organization that could bring extensive economic and social advantages to the EU population over a period of years. This is, of course, a tremendous challenge for the EU economic and social system, and accomplishment of this result may require many years. The time factor is uncertain, especially since it is difficult to predict how the states that will be admitted to the EU over the next 10 to 20 years will act and react in their new environment.

Progress toward integration of the EU will depend on a number of factors, perhaps most prominently the adoption of a common currency, the open flow of citizens across national boundaries, the improvement of the economic situation, and the insurance of a common foreign policy supported by a growing common military identity. William Wallace emphasized the importance of a sense of community, stressing that it involved the affective discussion of political integration.[1] The politicization of integration and its expansion into sensitive political space necessitate renewed attention to the questions "who are we?" and "who belongs" to which political community, which are deeply problematic at a time when national political communities and European institutions are faced with questions of inclusion/exclusion. How are we to determine the answer to some of these issues? The public opinion surveys conducted by the Commission are helpful and may indicate the trends of attitudes of the EU population, but drawing definite conclusions regarding the regional integration process remains difficult. The fact that the Maastricht Treaty establishes a "citizenship of the Union," under which each "person holding the nationality of a Member State" shall enjoy the rights conferred by this Treaty but also "shall be subject to the duties imposed thereby" (Article 8), raises difficult questions that produce uncertainties in the evaluation and interpretation of public opinion surveys on support for European unification, benefits from EU membership, the situation of the economy in the year to come, and the labor market in one's own country.[2]

We mentioned in a preceding chapter the use of regionalism in certain member states to enhance the possibility of European unification.[3] In the 1960s, the resurgence of regional political and cultural movements was noted in Scotland, Wales, Brittany, Corsica, Catalonia, and the Basque country.[4] More recently, the Italians became interested in setting up a federation with emphasis on Sicily and Northwest Italy, but so far the necessary constitutional changes have not been made. The German States of the Federation have also shown considerable interest in exerting influence on the decision-making process in the EU and have a number of representatives in Brussels. Similar actions have been taken by Scottish governmental agencies in Brussels. The Committee of the Regions—established to give opinions on regional issues—has been active, but whether this institution can contribute to moving the EU toward a federalized structure cannot be predicted at this time. Nevertheless, the number of regional representatives had increased from two in 1985 to 50 in 1994. The number of regional activities has grown, with the Association of European Regions and the Council of European Municipalities and Regions increasingly providing a transnational focus for regional and local communities since the mid-1980s. Europe's cities have joined the regions in the search for representation and networks beyond the borders of their states. In 1985 the Euro-Cities Association was founded by six cities; its membership in 1996 consisted of 38 cities.[5] These developments seem to have stressed regional identities and have broadened the politics of identity, leading many regions and cities to reevaluate where they are in Europe's emerging political and economic order. Some regional action highlights a vision of a "Europe of the Regions" in which the European nation states will dissolve in time. There is also a belief that a "Europe of the Regions" would be more democratic, efficient, and economically dynamic.[6]

But regardless of the constitutional and administrative structure of a potential European Union, the underlying economic and social bases that can be empirically determined must be taken into account to draw conclusions about the political future of the EU. As we have seen in chapter 4, economic growth during the last ten years was limited, and there was limited enthusiasm for the EU and the Maastricht Treaty to become the regional basis for decision making and implementation. Although the involvement of Eurocrats in these tasks is extensive, national civil servants also play a large role, and national concerns can find expression in the EU-national cooperation.

Another road to EU integration is the growth of regionalism espoused by increasing numbers of EU citizens, a primarily affective phenomenon but with underpinnings of economic interests. I have always felt that this route to integration, while relatively slow, may be effective because it weakens nationalistic tendencies among the populations in the EU and makes a different kind of constitutional system more acceptable over time, most probably several years.

If the unemployment situation should improve, this would add impetus to both utilitarian and affective motivation to move forward toward the EU, although it may not be sufficient to cause a majority of the EU population to accept a European federal constitutional operation—which may generate various political and legal problems.

Perhaps the most intriguing problem is the institution of a common currency which, if successful financially, could produce a more powerful economic Europe and provide financial gains for businesses and individuals. We discussed the possible consequences of starting the process of a common currency on time (Maastricht Treaty) in chapter 6; it is interesting to note that the management of various businesses and high-level banks see the powerful advantages of the European Monetary System and discuss various policies to ensure membership for their countries.[7] Spain and Italy made clear in October 1996 that they intend to do their utmost to qualify for the first round of monetary union in 1998–99. This will require special arrangements in their national budgets in 1997, the year on which eligibility will be judged. The president of the European Monetary Institute (EMI), who is slated to be the first president of the European Central Bank, stated that the move toward the EMU may well bring to European countries the possibilities of improving the functioning of their economies and higher employment, a problematic but hopeful area. On the other hand, dramatic political concerns have produced in Austria an electoral polarization toward anti-Europeanism, and in Sweden similar trends have been noted, although not caused by right-wing political forces as in Austria. The Bank of England has discussed setting up a high-level meeting or committee to discuss the relationship to EMU, but the election in May 1997, which produced a new make-up of the British government, is likely to change the relationship between the United Kingdom and its EU partners and produce appropriate decisions about the initial participation in the common currency. An IGC dealing with the future of the EU, including participation in EMU, is being held before the end of 1997, and may offer many insights into the exact time when the common currency begins and who can be a member. Indeed, even Germany, which was considered fully assured economically as a member of EMU, is being accused by a number of highly qualified domestic economic institutes as being in too great a rush in the introduction of the common currency and in overestimating its economic assets.[8]

What appears to be emerging from the dispute over the introduction of EMU is a severe struggle about not only the currency issue but also progress of the EU integration process. British policy before the election was to insist on individual governmental choice of member states without concern about the future fate of the Union. This has changed, and the new prime minister has even declared that Britain will sign the EU social charter, from which the conservative government had opted out. Considering that the number of members soon may increase to 25, with some of the candidates uncertain whether they want to accept the possible restrictions of the EU,[9] the future, including that of the EMU, looks somewhat difficult. However, part of the population anticipates some success, economic and social, when the IGC reports its results—a limited anticipation that is also reflected in the *Eurobarometer* findings. The actual move to the Euro beginning in 1999 also requires a good amount of discretion and care, including the challenge of calculation by the public to determine the Euro and local currency rates for exchange purposes. Undoubtedly, even in Germany, strong efforts will be made to stop the march to the Euro, but the Commission is convinced that it will be launched in January 1999, although not all EU states may then be members of EMU.[10]

While there are many reasons to support further regional integration in the present and future EU, the slowly growing opposition was evident in the public opinion chapter. To overcome the pervasive nationalist tendencies attempting to block the acceptance of a decision-making structure that is more supportive of majority voting and more effective of regional implementation would require affective and utilitarian progress toward a federal system. Slowing of movement in this direction has been a recurrent phenomenon in the European Community since the Treaties of Rome were fully implemented at the end of the 1960s. Despite quarterly meetings of the Commission and the ministers of the member states, and despite many suggestions to enhance the task performance of the European structures, little progress has been made beyond the initiation of the SEA.

Perhaps for an outside observer it is best to stick with an intergovernmental background in order to explain the present and predict the future. This means that regional integration of the EU will be very slow and that common foreign policy and military cooperation of the member states will be quite stagnant, as majority voting remains a dream at present. A recent example was the implementation of a maximum 48-hour work week, which came before the European Court of Justice and was strongly resisted by the last U.K. government. If the judgment had gone against the United Kingdom, its government threatened to veto any reform proposed at the current IGC, and this would have ended any prospect of improving the operation of the EU under the Maastricht Treaty.[11] If the spirit of democracy were to permeate EU activities in the future, as discussed in chapter 3, progress in integration may be possible, especially with the Blair U.K. government's attitude, as previously discussed, which may inspire pro-EU declarations in other member states and enhance the democratic spirit and with it the potential success of the IGC and EMU.

A broad emotional commitment by EU member states to the concept of closer cooperation would possibly overcome to some extent the basic anti-federalist and pro-nationalist attitudes of the participants. It may lead to interpretations of such principles as subsidiarity in a more positive manner and, even under difficult circumstances, lead to the positive application of this principle. At the same time, it is interesting to note that if we look at the constitutional future and the evolving administrative structure of the EU, highest priority must be given to the achievement of the basic task objective of EU unity.

What can be seen from the *Financial Times*[12] is a conflict of opinions among members of the EU, national governments, and lower levels of state authority about how to proceed with the IGC, what changes should be made to the Maastricht Treaty, or whether it would be best to abandon the whole enterprise. The future enlargement of the EU has emphasized the tremendous difficulty of change and adaptations that the supporters of the Commission want to realize, but which the opposition considers foolish.[13] The conflicting arguments have drawn on current events. The foreign minister of Ireland, in early November 1996, emphasized that the hoped-for enlargement of the EU in Eastern Europe will not be possible until the existing members can agree on new rules at their ongoing Intergovernmental Conference (IGC). He expressed concern at that time that the British government, and to a lesser degree, the Danish government were not prepared to negotiate a compromise to reach agreement in the talks with the other 13 EU members. "There must be enlargement when we get the IGC right." He promised that the Irish government would present applicable drafts for the EU summit in December 1996 proposing institutional reforms and pertaining to foreign and security policy. Considering the basic contractual need for agreement, the prospects were slim; and they darkened further when the East European peculiarities were taken into account.

ADDENDUM

Following the Irish failure to finalize the IGC, it was up to the European Union presidency of the Netherlands during the first six months of 1997 to find an appropriate conclusion. With the British elections of May 1 supporting Labour and the new prime minister, Tony Blair, taking a much more sympathetic attitude toward the EU (although he insists on maintaining British interests foremost),[14] the potential for completing the IGC has improved. One of the main tasks of the conference is reform of EU institutions so they can cope better with more members. Other points are the size, structure, and role of the European Commission to deal effectively with enlargement and to change the voting procedures in the Council of Ministers. Both topics are politically sensitive and may be influenced by the elections for the French National Assembly called by President Chirac on May 25 and June 1. The result of this election was a socialist government under the premiership of Lionel Jospin and with Communist Party minority participation. Clearly, the common currency issue was a key factor in these elections, but the potential future advantages in the economic arena that also may affect social concerns favorably may be attractive. When the IGC was operating under the Dutch presidency in the first half of 1997, the Heads of State and Government adopted what came to be known as the Treaty of Amsterdam. Its purpose was to make the European Union more effective and more democratic, but it was uncertain whether these aims were being achieved. If the problem of the IGC cannot be unraveled by the Dutch efforts, Luxembourg's EU presidency will be called upon to find an acceptable solution during the last six months of 1997. These IGC delays may not necessarily upset the common currency timetable, but the solution of the IGC problem would give the progress of the EU plans a definite boost. However, the

September 1997 meeting of the EU finance minister and central bankers in Luxembourg regarding the Euro was much more positive and strengthened the potential for a successful common currency in 1999.

NOTES

[1]Brigid Laffan, "The Politics of Identity and Political Order in Europe," *Journal of Common Market Studies* 34, no. 1 (March 1996), p. 83.

[2]*Eurobarometer* 45 (Spring 1996), p. VI.

[3]See Laffan. "The Politics of Identity," pp. 88–101, and Werner J. Feld, with John K. Wildgen, "Italy and European Unification," in *Il Politico* XXXIX, pp. 334–48.

[4]Ibid.

[5]See Laffan, "The Politics of Identity," p. 91.

[6]Ibid., pp. 90–91.

[7]For detailed discussion on the issues see *Financial Times*, 29 October, 1996, p. 2.

[8]*Financial Times*, 30 October, 1996, p. 1, and *New York Times*, 4 April, 1997, pp. A1–A8, which stated that Chancellor Kohl would run for an unprecedented fifth four-year term in 1998 to champion closer European unity despite current high unemployment in Germany. This was a follow-up to another article in the *Financial Times* on 29 October, 1996, p. 2, quoting the governor of the Dutch Central Bank that the path to the single currency relied too much on "budgetary maneuvers."

[9]The newly elected prime minister of Malta, to be an EU member by the end of the century, is "anti-EU" (*Financial Times*, 31 October, 1996, p. 2).

[10]See *Infeuro*, no. 2 (March 1997).

[11]See *Financial Times*, 1 November, 1996, p. 1, for details.

[12]9 November, 1996, pp. 2, 3, 7, and 24 September 1997, p.2.

[13]Ibid.

[14]*Financial Times*, 11 May, 1997, p. 4.

SELECTED BIBLIOGRAPHY

Carmeron, David R. "The 1992 Initiative: Causes and Consequences." In *Euro-Politics*, edited by Alberta M. Skragia. Washington, DC: The Brookings Institution, 1991.

Chryssochoou, Dimitris N. Paper presented at the ECSA Conference, Charleston, SC: May 1995.

Colorado Springs Gazette Telegraph, 23 July, 1996.

Commission Report, *Intergovernmental Conference*, 1996.

Commission Report for the Reflection Group *Intergovernmental Conference 1996*.

The Courier, no. 155, January-February 1996. "Special Issue on the Revised Lomé Convention."

Dentsch, Karl W. *Political Community and the North Atlantic Area*. Princeton, NJ: Princeton University Press, 1957.

Denver Post, Denver, CO.

Eurecom.

Eurobarometer 45 (Spring 1996).

European Agence International, Europe Documents no. 96, 10 May, 1996.

European Commission. *The European Council: Decision-Making in European Politics*. London: Macmillan, 1987.

European Commission. *European Economy*, Supplement A, Economic Trends, no. 12 (December 1995).

European Union News, July 16, 1997, no. 49/97.

Feld, Werner J. *The European Community in World Affairs*. New York: Alfred Publishing Co., 1976.

Feld, Werner J. *The Future of European Security and Defense Policy.* Boulder, CO: Lynne Rienner Publishers, 1992.

Feld, Werner J., with John K. Wildgen. "Italy and European Unification." In *Il Politico* XXXIX.

Financial Times.

Ginsburg, Roy H. *Foreign Policy Actions of the European Community.* Boulder, CO: Lynne Rienner Publishers, 1989.

Groom, R. J. A. "The European Commonality Building Up, Breaking Down, and Building Across." *Conference Proceedings, People's Rights and European Structures,* Centro Unesco de Catalunya, 1993.

Groom, A. J. R., and Paul Taylor, eds. "Consocialionalism and Federalism as Approaches to International Integration." In *Frameworks for International Cooperation.* New York: St. Martin's Press, 1990.

Haas, Ernst R. "The Obsolescence of Regional Integration Theory." *Institute of International Studies* Research Series 25, Berkeley, University of California, 1975.

Haas, Ernst R. *The Uniting of Europe.* Stanford, CA: Stanford University Press, 1955.

Inglehart, Ronald. *The Silent Revolution.* Princeton, NJ: Princeton University Press, 1977.

Intergovernmental Conference 1996, the Commission Report for the Reflection Group, Annex 17.

International Herald Tribune.

Keohane, Robert D. *Power and Interdependence: World Politics in Transition.* Boston: Little, Brown, 1977.

Kirchner, Emil. *Decision Making in the European Community.* Manchester and New York: Manchester University Press, 1992.

Laffan, Brigid. "The Politics of Identity and Political Order in Europe." *Journal of Common Market Studies* 34, no. 1 (March 1996).

Lindberg, Leon N. *The Political Dynamics of European Economic Integration.* Stanford, CA: Stanford University Press, 1963.

London Times, London, England.

Maastricht Treaty on European Union, "Protocol on the European Monetary Institute" (EMI).

Mahler, Vincent, Bruce Taylor, and Jennifer Wozinak, "Exploring the Relationship Between Economic Growth and Public Attitudes Toward European Integration." Paper presented at the ECSA Conference, Charleston, SC: 11–14 May, 1995.

Mazey, Sonia, and Jeremy Richardson. "Pressure Groups and Lobbying in the EC." *The European Community and the Challenge of the Future* 2nd ed., edited by Juliet Lodge. New York: St. Martin's Press, 1993.

Mitrany, David. *A Working Peace System.* Chicago: Quadrangle Books, 1966.

Morarscik, Andrew. "Preference and Power in the European Community: A Liberal Intergovernmentalist Approach." *Journal of Common Market Studies* 31, no. 4 (December 1993).

Moxon-Browne, Edward. "Social Europe." in *The European Community and the Challenge of the Future,* 2nd ed., edited by Juliet Lodge. New York: St. Martin's Press, 1993.

New York Times, New York, NY.

Nugent, Neill. *The Government and Politics of the European Community* 2nd ed. Durham, NC: Duke University Press, 1991.

Pentland, Charles. *International Theory and European Integration*. New York: The Free Press, 1973.

Puchala, Donald. "International Transactions and Regional Integration." *International Organization* 24, 1970.

Schmitter, Philip C. "A Revised Theory of Regional Integration." *International Organization* 24, no. 4 (Autumn 1970).

Tovias, Alfred. "A Survey of the Theory of Economic Integration." In *European Integration,* edited by H.J. Michelman and Panayotis Soldatos. New York: The Free Press, 1973.

Wessels, Wolfgang. "New Forms of Foreign Policy Formulation in Western Europe." In *Western Europe's Global Reach,* edited by Werner J. Feld. NY: Pergamon Press.

Wooley, John T. "Policy Credibility and European Monetary Institutions." In *Euro-Politics*, edited by Alberta M. Skragia. Washington, DC: The Brookings Institution, 1991.

Young, Oran R. "International Regimes: Problems of Concept Formation." *World Politics* 32 (April 1980).

INDEX

About the Author

WERNER J. FELD is Adjunct Professor of Political Science at the University of Colorado, Colorado Springs. Professor Feld's long and distinguished career centered on the University of New Orleans, where he taught for many years and authored, coauthored, or edited more than 20 books.

ISBN 0-275-96068-4

HARDCOVER BAR CODE